The IRON Butterfly

Memoir of a Martial Arts Master

The True Story of a Mermaid's Daughter

CHOON-OK JADE HARMON
WITH ANA MARÍA RODRÍGUEZ

PELICAN PUBLISHING COMPANY
GRETNA 2011

To Kuk Sa Nim and Chief Master, who changed my life. To all of my family, whose support brought me where I am today. And to my husband and daughters, who convinced me to tell my story. —Choon-Ok Harmon

To José, Frankie, and Marcos, my husband and sons, who walk along with me in my writer's journey. —Ana María Rodríguez

The word "Pelican" and the depiction of a pelican are trademarks of Pelican Publishing Company, Inc., and are registered in the U.S. Patent and Trademark Office.

Library of Congress Cataloging-in-Publication Data

Harmon, Choon-Ok Jade.
Rodríguez, Ana María.
   The Iron Butterfly : memoir of a martial arts master / Choon-Ok Jade Harmon with Ana María Rodríguez.
      p. cm.
   Includes bibliographical references and index.
   ISBN 978-1-58980-890-4 (hardcover : alk. paper) 1. Biography & Autobiography–Sports
   E470.7.B57 2010
   976.2'05–dc22
                              2010029019

Printed in the United States of America
Published by Pelican Publishing Company, Inc.
1000 Burmaster Street, Gretna, Louisiana 70053

Contents

The IRON Butterfly

Memoir of a Martial Arts Master

Introduction

Before I Tell You My Story

On a cold March morning, I decided to tell my story. It was one of the hardest decisions of my life. Just think about it. Telling your personal story is not what Koreans do, especially Korean women of my generation. We don't tell everybody about our misfortunes, poverty, or good times. Writing a book about my life story would be just that—telling my story to anybody willing to read it. Once it's out there anybody can read it. That was very hard for me to come to terms with.

I worry that my Korean family will be angry at me for writing my story, which includes them sometimes. I truly love all my family and respect them and I would never want to hurt them or make them angry. But still, I have decided to tell my story. I hope they understand that, in the twenty-first century, it's all right to do this. People are more open and write their stories, the good and the bad, showing others what they have learned from their experiences. But this is not easy for me. I also don't want to leave the impression that all Korean men would make bad husbands. I have known many who are not. But I had my reasons not to marry a Korean man. My story reflects my unique, personal experiences and desires in life. It is not my intention to offend anybody. I respect all men; I just wanted a different life for myself.

I understand that our lives are private—that we just share them with our mothers, sisters, children, and spouses. The less other people know about us, the better. Besides, who would be interested in knowing about my hard times when I was a little girl living on a small island? Who would like to know the octopus story or hear about my closest encounter with death? Who would like to know what my true-life martial arts training was all about? Or know of my struggles in Pusan or of my culture clashes in America? Or read about people constantly challenging my ability to stand up for myself? Who would like to know of my temper or of my suffering when my daughters were ill? All these reasons weighed heavily against me telling my story, but there was a counterbalance that outweighed my fears about my family and going against my Korean nature.

My husband tells me my story is worth telling. It is very different from what most people go through in America. He tells me that people would like to know what I did to change my life, from barely surviving in Koje Do Island during the post-Korean War era to living in America with my American husband and our two daughters, in my own house. People would like to know what it takes to become the first woman to achieve the highest rank in the Korean Martial Art of Kuk Sool Won. Still, I was not convinced.

But then, here come my daughters. I have told some of my stories to Emerald and Jada and they are very surprised when they hear them. *"Wow!"* they say. "In spite of all that happened to you, you made it!" They are amazed how their world, and my world when I was their age, could be so different. There is a big contrast between living in a small Korean island in the 1960s and living in the suburb of an American city in the twenty-first century. "You have to tell your stories," they say. I thought about my daughters and what they said about my stories for years.

Koreans tell their stories and keep them alive for generations by oral tradition. Mothers tell their stories to their daughters and they in time pass them on to their own daughters. Nothing is preserved on paper, just in memories. But we live in America now, and here the written tradition predominates oral tradition. Maybe I have to move on with the new times and the place where I live now. Maybe I have to put all my stories in writing to preserve them for my family's future generations.

I have another reason for writing my life story; the process will help me come to terms with many difficult issues, to understand them better, and to understand myself better. Life has been hard and left scars on me, but I want to make the best of my life experiences, and putting them in writing will help me achieve that goal.

It took me a long time to decide, but I have made up my mind. I will tell my story. I want it to be available for my daughters, my grandchildren, and great-grandchildren to read it when they want to know about the experiences that made me who I am today. It's my gift to them. If others read them, it's OK with me. I have made my decision.

Now I have a new concern. How would I begin my story? My story begins in 1956 in a small fishing village in the southern Korean island of

Koje Do. Three years had passed since the Korean War had come to an end. Land and families were still recovering slowly from the devastation and tragedies of the war. One of those families was mine, the Lee family. I was going to join them, but my arrival would add more weight to their already heavy family load. I was not welcomed. This is how it all began.

PART ONE

LIVING IN AN ISLAND
OF MERMAIDS

Chapter 1

Haenyo, the Sea Woman

At the darkest hour of the night, just before dawn, my mother and my sister got ready to leave the house. It was freezing cold, but the only thing my mother, Pak Ung-Ak, could do was to wrap her thin body in an old jacket and make sure she brought with her all she needed for her journey. She reached for a "bahk," a dried, hollow gourd about the size of a basketball, and tied it to a long mesh bag making a "do ru bahk." She grabbed her goggles, another mesh bag, and a home-made knife, and stepped out into the freezing darkness. "Bring me the do ru bahk," Mom called to her fourteen-year-old daughter, my sister Jung-Ja. Jung-Ja also wrapped herself up in a hand-me-down coat, picked up the do ru bahk, and followed Mom, shivering. It was so dark they could barely see what was in front of them, but it didn't matter much. They knew the way.

Woman and child walked side by side on the narrow dirt path. Their only companions were the soothing sounds of the ocean waves and Mom's humming of old haenyo songs. Mom was going to dive in the ocean; she was a haenyo (Hey-in-*yuh*), or a "sea woman." People say that haenyo are like mermaids, because they spend so much time every day diving in the ocean. They deep dive to harvest seaweed, shells, octopus, abalone, sea urchin, and other animal and vegetable life for food and sale. Mom had learned this traditional Korean woman's task as a child and now, at forty years of age, she was still at it, regardless of how severe the weather conditions were or how pregnant she might be.

For about three hours they walked fast, trying to keep their slim bodies warm. Sometimes, they had to slow down. Mom was carrying a new life, me, in her body, and I was almost ready to enter the world. But it didn't matter to Mom that the time had almost come for the baby to be born. She had to do what she had to do to keep her family alive. She had to dive and find food for herself and her family at the bottom of the ocean, and hopefully have some left to sell and earn a meager income. One of the most striking aspects of haenyo is that they dive without any breathing equipment. They do not use an oxygen tank or flippers. Their strength comes from their trained lungs and iron will. I learned years later that haenyo could dive to about fifty feet deep just with the air inhaled in one deep breath before submerging, and they could hold their breath for a few minutes while looking for food.

Mom did not wear the diving suits haenyo wear today; she dove wearing cotton trunks and a black shirt. On top, she wore a long-sleeve, white shirt tied under her breast. She tied her long, black hair, wore goggles, and carried a knife and a do ru bahk. Mom spent hours in the ocean taking breaks between minute-long dives. She used the hollowed bahk as a flotation device. Every time she swam back up to the surface, Mom wrapped her arms around the bahk, pulling it into her chest, and rested, catching her breath before diving again. In the mesh bag that hung underwater from the bahk, Mom stored the food she had gathered during dives.

Mom and Jung-Ja reached their favorite diving spot just as the sun was rising. Mom liked this place because the ocean was calm and there were no strong currents that would carry the unanchored do ru bahk far away from her. It would usually stay floating close to where she had placed it at the beginning of her dive, and she could find it easily every time she swam back to the surface to refill her lungs with much-needed air. She also preferred this spot because it was so far away from the village that few haenyo used it, leaving more for Mom to harvest.

Mom took her jacket off, tied the do ru bahk to her waist, and slowly climbed down a steep, rugged, broken cliff, holding on to the boulders with both hands. Mom was at the end of the pregnancy; birth could happen any time now. She told me years later that when she stood next to the freezing water, looking down at the deep, dark ocean, she felt fear of diving for the first time. Then, she looked up at the rising sun. She knew she had no choice. She had to dive. If she didn't, nobody would feed her children waiting at home.

Ignoring the freezing temperatures of mid-February, Mom adjusted the goggles around her eyes, grabbed the knife in one hand, threw the do ru bahk into the water, and tied a mesh cloth bag to her waist. She took a few deep breaths, closed her eyes, and slowly submerged her pregnant body into the dark, icy water. She told my sister Jung-Ja later that as the freezing water engulfed her body, she felt the mind-numbing cold pour into her joints as if the freezing water had seeped beneath her skin itself. But this weakening feeling did not stop Mom. She had to get food for the family.

Jung-Ja waited patiently at the edge of the cliff, crouching behind a boulder that shielded her from the chilling wind, rubbing her hands and blowing warm breath into them. Once she had warmed up, she left her shielded place and gathered firewood. She started a fire to keep herself warm and to warm up Mom when she came out of the water. Mom was teaching Jung-Ja how to be a haenyo, just like Mom's mother had taught her when she was young. The tradition has been passed from mother to daughter in Korea for hundreds of years. Jung-Ja dove during the warmer seasons, and in winter it was her job to tend the fire when Mom had to dive.

Below, in the dimly lit ocean, Mom looked for what she had come for. There it was—seaweed. She reached for it but missed it. She tried again and got a hold of it, but it was so slippery that she lost her grip. Her sight was blurry, she felt lightheaded, and the birth contractions began. She ignored the pain. She had come for food and she would get it. Her four children had to eat. If she didn't get anything today, there would be no food on the table.

She swam back to the surface to catch a fresh breath of air. The do ru bahk was still floating where she had placed it. She wrapped her arms around it, resting her face on its smooth surface. Slowly, she exhaled, producing a controlled, long whistling sound all haenyo learned to make. She floated effortlessly while breathing deeply to recover her strength and ease the birth pain. Jung-Ja saw her and wondered if something was wrong, but before she could ask, Mom dove into the ocean again.

This time, Mom had decided to try to collect sea urchin or abalone, but another pang hit her weakened body; she hadn't eaten a solid meal in days. The pain was stronger. She could not ignore the message any longer.

With resignation, Mom swam to the surface. She wrapped her arms around the do ru bahk and slowly kicked her legs, swimming toward land. She climbed up the cliff and met Jung-Ja by the fire. Jung-Ja pointed at Mom's hair. It was sparkling with icicles. That's how cold it was.

"Out so soon?" asked Jung-Ja surprised.

"We have to go home. The baby is coming," Mom said.

After the comforting fire had removed the chill from Mom's bones, mother and child extinguished the fire and walked back home as quickly as they could. I, her seventh child, was coming and there was no stopping me. Only four children lived with her then: her oldest son had died and her oldest daughter lived in another city.

They had not even walked half the way back when Mom had another contraction. She gasped for air, kneeled slowly on the dirt path, and then lay on the ground, screaming in pain; the contractions were so strong she could do nothing else. Jung-Ja did not know how to help. She kneeled beside her, caressing her head and arms. Maybe she encouraged her to continue walking, but Jung-Ja does not remember; she was just fourteen years old and did not know what to do except comfort Mom. When the pain became tolerable, Mom got back on her feet and continued walking, slowly this time. As they approached home, Mom had to stop and lie down more often; the contractions now seemed to be just minutes apart.

They had to stop so many times that it took Mom and Jung-Ja four hours instead of three to reach home. Mom was exhausted after the dive and the long walk. She collapsed on her bed and hoped for nature to take its course. But there was no strength left in her to push me out.

Chapter 2

Rough Beginnings

My mom was very unhappy when I was born. My home was in one of the many villages that had sprouted on Koje Do Island. Koje Do is the second largest island of Korea, second to Cheju Island. My island is just a 40-minute boat ride from Pusan in the mainland. But in my mother's time before I was born, the trip by boat took the whole day. To reach our neighbor Japan, Mom had to travel several days by boat.

My family name is Lee and we lived in a small, two-room house with a thatched roof. The back of our home faced a mountain. The ragged mountain had many trees and beautiful flowers that colored the mountainside from spring to fall. The mountain also had many rocks and boulders, and fresh, cold, narrow creeks that snaked down from the cropped heights. I have lost count of how many times I climbed this mountain and watched the sunrise or the sunset. The view was captivating; I could have stayed there for hours, just admiring what I saw.

The smooth ocean was within walking distance of the front of my home, and it created a powerful contrast with the rugged mountain behind it. The calm and swaying sea seemed to soothe the rough mountain edges, but I would never have traded the mountain for the ocean. In the mountain, I felt safe. I knew the mountain. I knew where to find every tree with strong branches to climb. I knew every creek rushing with cold, sparkling water to calm my thirst. I knew the best places to go to try my slingshot my brother Choon-Duk taught me to build. I could see everything.

It was different with the ocean. I know I should feel thankful for having an ocean that provided us with food. I should be thankful the ocean did not take my mom away after she took so much food from it. But I don't trust the ocean. It is so turbid I can never see the bottom. I don't know if I can touch bottom or not. I don't know what lies beneath. The ocean is a mystery. I prefer the open mountain. I feel that mountains

Model of a Korean house, such as the one in which Choon-Ok lived in Koje Do.

can be trusted, because they don't change much with the passing of time. My modest home faced the mysterious ocean and was guarded by an eternal mountain at its back. Here I was born and lived the first nine years of my life.

My home was one of about one hundred small thatch-roofed homes in a village dedicated, for the most part, to fishing. Some villagers, like my Mom, also earned an income trading with the mainland and our Japanese neighbors, but the majority of my village's business was with the sea.

Men and women alike were attracted to fishing: the sea business. Many, like Mom, felt a debt of gratitude for all that the sea had given them without apparently receiving anything in return. Mom dove to bring home seaweed, abalone, octopus, sea urchin, and other sea life. She sold all she could and we ate what was left. When my sister Jung-Ja, who was also a haenyo, grew up, she helped her family the same way Mom helped ours. But diving brought her misfortune. I never dived. I never learned to swim until I was an adult. I did not need it until later in life.

I was a late addition to my family, unexpected and unwelcome. When it was my time to join them, my parents already had four young mouths to feed. Those mouths were rarely full in those days. It was not just our family. Others in the village also had a hard time making a living. The effects of the Korean War were felt for a long time. When I was born, in 1956, three years after the war had ended, our land and people were still struggling to recover. For many Koreans, food was scarce and winter nights were very cold.

It is not that my parents were lazy, sick, or too weak to work. I have never seen anybody work as hard as my mom. Sometimes, she told me, things went well and she could earn quite a big sum of money between her job as a haenyo and the trading business. During those times, which my family enjoyed before I was born, food was abundant at the table. There would be fish, chicken, kimchi, many vegetables, and rice. My brothers and sisters would have new clothes, which were bought in Pusan more often than once a year for their birthdays. My mom even saved some money. She always worked hard and put her kids' and her husband's needs before her own. But not my father. Dad's name was Lee Kyung-Ju.

Like many Koreans, the Lees had two names. My father's name, Kyung-Ju, which means "respect," was the name he commonly used, but his registered name was Lee, Dohl-Ri. Dohl-Ri means "stone" in Korean. My father used his registered name for legal documents, but he used Kyung-Ju on all other occasions because he liked that name more. The registered names of my mom and my siblings are the ones I mention in my story. My father gave me the name Chu Ja, when I was born, but I did not like it because it means "walnut." I pleaded to Mom to change it and when it was time to register me to attend school, she asked me if I would like to go by Choon-Ok, which means "Spring Jade." I loved what Choon-Ok means and I was happy to have a pretty name.

Mom said Dad was spoiled. She thought so because he didn't have to work when he was young, like she did. He never learned to work. My paternal grandfather was a government official, but I'm not sure exactly what kind and where. His job provided a good income and they also had land and other properties, so my dad's family did not need him to work to provide for the family. They could afford to send him to school. But my father did not go to school; he enjoyed the many pleasures of life instead. He gambled, and he drank. "He was spoiled," said Mom. "Never marry a man like him," was her advice.

Because he was spoiled when he was young, Mom reasoned, he continued living the same kind of life after he married her. That's what he was used to and what he liked. He did not know or want anything different. It was not quite what Mom had expected. But anyway, in Mom's time women could only speculate about what type of husband they would have. Until not long ago, Korean women did not choose their husbands; their parents decided who they would marry. Arranged marriages did not come with a guarantee of happiness and a good spouse. My family could live with my father's carelessness while fortune favored my mom's work. But when misfortune knocked at our door and his bad habits did not change, our life became very difficult.

Korean families tended to have many children at that time, and mine was not an exception. By 1955, Mom had already had six children; three boys and three girls. Of the six Lee siblings, the oldest boy had passed away when he was very young. Feeding and dressing five hungry mouths was getting harder every day. Because my father didn't provide any kind of income, the load was heavier on Mom. The war situation made it harder to earn a living; jobs did not come easily. Meals became smaller and less frequent. Coal was scarce in the house during winter. Winter nights felt bitter cold and harder to endure no matter how tightly my sisters cuddled with Mom in the family bed. The last thing Mom wanted was one more mouth to feed, but that was what life brought her. She couldn't believe that her situation could get any worse, but it did. She decided to avoid having another child at all costs.

Four and a half years after her last child was born—my brother Choon-Duk—Mom discovered that she was pregnant again. She could not believe it at first, but after three months of missing her period, called "Whol Gyung" in Korean, or the "Moon's Blood Course," she was convinced; she was expecting a child again.

I can understand her feelings now and her desire to end the pregnancy, but I don't know what I would have done in her place. She had the responsibility to care for two sons (Hwa-Nam and Choon-Duk) and two daughters (Jung-Ja and Choon-Up), besides feeding my father and herself. My oldest sister, Choon-Ja, had moved to Seoul so Mom didn't need to take care of her.

"What was I suppose to do?" she told me years later. "I already couldn't feed your brothers and sisters, and a new baby was on the way." There was no doubt that a new baby would make it harder on the others. Mom told me that she resolved to try anything she could think of to terminate the pregnancy.

There were not many medical means she could use. They would

cost money, and there was no money left after she bought food for the family. But her imagination was fertile and she came up with a few unconventional ideas—some might even seem funny now that many years have passed—but they were futile attempts to end a growing life. Mom's attempts only confirmed how resilient life can be.

She tried to abort by rolling down the mountain many times. Her thin and fragile body rolled down the rocks, leaving bumps and bruises on her arms and legs. But all the injuries were on her. I, who was only a small lump of life, embraced existence relentlessly and refused to give it up. "Rolling down the mountain didn't work," Mom told me.

She then turned to the village grandmothers in search of old remedies that would quickly end my brief life. The village grandmothers recommended drinking very old soy sauce. Not the "fresh" one-year-old soy sauce that tastes good, but the repugnant, six- or seven-year-old stuff nobody likes because it tastes so bad. They assured her that it would make her lose the baby. "I drank that awful soy sauce," Mom told me. But nothing happened. I continued holding on to my life, leaving Mom disappointed and with a bad taste in her mouth.

If you could describe Mom in one word, it would be persistent. She did not stop there; she tried one more technique. She squeezed her abdomen, pressed hard on it with her hands, and folded it in futile attempts to push me out of her body. She tried for weeks unsuccessfully. At the end, she was disappointed again, and dark bruises covered her abdomen. I, on the other hand, had won my first battle in life. I continued growing and Mom had no choice but to accept me. She was going to have another mouth to feed.

Many years later, when I was in my twenties, I asked Mom, "Why?" Why did she let it happen? I was so angry! "Why did you sleep with father when our family was going through difficult times?" I asked one night. We were together, alone, at home, getting ready to go to sleep. I cried when I asked her the question, looking straight into her eyes. If she didn't want more children, why did she let it happen? I could not understand it.

She did not answer. She did not look me in the eye. She didn't want to talk about it, I could tell, but I had to know. I kept asking her the same question; I insisted, trying to hold my tears back, but my voice broke. I always had so many questions for her. I needed to understand why things were the way they were. She must have realized that I would never stop asking her questions unless she answered me. She screamed, "OK!" and talked to me.

"I refused to sleep with your dad many times. I pushed him away because I knew how hard it would be on the family if I got pregnant again. I pushed him away all but one time. Just one time! And here you are, because of one time." We laughed together. "You were meant to be. I am very happy that you were born because you have been a very good daughter." Mom would never know how happy I was when I heard those last words after we had had so many confrontations.

The family's situation did not improve during Mom's pregnancy; it actually grew worse with each passing week. Father did not help; Mom had to work constantly, carrying a load that just got heavier and heavier by the week, and winter was settling in for the villagers of Koje Do. In February of 1956, Mom's last pregnancy reached full term and I was born.

The delivery was very difficult. Mom and Jung-Ja had finally arrived home after walking for four hours in very cold, windy weather. The walk back home had been very stressful, because the contractions were increasingly frequent and Mom had to lie down on the ground until they passed.

Once they arrived home, Mom was so tired that she had little strength left in her to deliver the baby. My sister did not know what to do. She looked at Mom. Dad was not around, so Jung-Ja appealed to the neighbors. A caring neighbor had seen Mom and Jung-Ja getting back home. She probably saw Mom slouching and holding her big abdomen with one hand and supporting her body on my sister's shoulder with her other hand.

Mom lay in her bed and clasped the covers, trying to ease the pain. I was ready to enter this world. I needed a little help from Mom, but she did not have enough strength to push. She tried for many hours but couldn't push me out. Mom only had enough strength to cry and scream. My sister Jung-Ja didn't know what to do. She went outside, crying. Our neighbor, Mom's friend, saw her and asked if the baby had arrived.

Jung-Ja said that the baby had not arrived yet because Mom was too weak to push. She had not eaten a solid meal in days. Mom's friend walked around the village and told the neighbors there was an emergency at our home. Mom needed food to recover enough of her strength to give birth. The neighbors helped. Mom's friend collected a bowl of rice and gave it to Jung-Ja. Jung-Ja boiled the rice and brought the rice water to Mom.

Mom was resting on the mattress with her eyes closed, breathing slowly. Jung-Ja lifted Mom's head and touched her lips with the rim of the bowl of warm rice water. Mom drank a small sip of the water. She took more sips until half the water was gone. A few minutes passed. A few more. The warm rice water gave Mom some nourishment, and labor slowly resumed its normal course. A few more minutes passed and Mom was able to push. What happened later is a blur in my sister's memory. I was born and Mom slowly recovered her strength thanks to the rice and other foods the neighbors brought later.

Mom said that she could not believe how much energy a small bit of rice water had given her. It was enough for me to be born. The next day, Mom's friend came to visit; she wanted to see the baby that had caused Mom so much trouble. When she took one look at me, she told Mom, "Wow! She's such a small, skinny baby. How could she give you such a hard time? I could have farted one time and pushed this little thing out of me!" My mom and her friend had a good laugh together.

Dad came to see us, Mom told me. He said, "Uhm, a girl." He turned his face away from me and left the room. He did not look at me. He asked Mom something like, "What use is another girl?" All this made her very sad. Her husband did not even look at their baby! Dad would not look at me or hold me in his arms until I was three years old.

Without saying one word, Mom wrapped me in a hand-me-down blanket and put me by her side. She breast fed me, hugged me, and kept me warm. Three days later, still bleeding, Mom went back to diving. Nothing had changed. She had to find food for my brothers and sisters; nobody else would. She already knew this was going to happen and was resigned to do it.

Mom feared something might happen to me. Dad was not only disappointed that I was a girl, but he saw me as an unnecessary burden for the family. Mom was worried, even scared, because she had heard of other families throwing their baby daughters into the ocean shortly after they were born. Girls were poorly regarded, and some families thought it was only fair to the rest of the family to discard baby girls when times were tough. Some families preferred boys, because they were in short supply after the war. Mom did not think that way, and this might have saved my life.

Mom knew Dad's feelings about baby girls and she was afraid that he might throw me into the ocean one day when he came home drunk and frustrated and she was not there to protect me. She did not want this to happen. She regarded life highly, regardless of its gender. She decided to protect me from Dad. She did not want to leave me at home in my sister's care and come back one day to find that Dad had taken me, never to return. There was only one way Mom could make sure I would be safe.

Mom took me with her everywhere she went. She placed me on her back and bundled us together with a long blanket made out of cloth called "po dae gi." It was the traditional Korean way mothers carried their babies, and Mom was going to carry me all day long. We were always together—when she slept; when she was cleaning the house, cooking, or shopping; and when she was singing or humming soothing tunes. I even accompanied her on her diving trips.

Mom resumed diving shortly after I was born. Now both Jung-Ja and I accompanied her on her diving trips. When Mom was ready to dive, she removed me from her back, wrapped me in a blanket, and placed me between two big rocks so I would not roll down and fall into the ocean. Sometimes, Mom placed a small, flat rock over me, supported by the two rocks on my sides, to shield me from the wind.

Jung-Ja looked for wood, made a fire, and kept it burning to keep us warm. Mom told me that I was a quiet baby most of the time, but once I began crying so loudly that she could hear me even though she was under water! On that occasion, she thought, "What am I doing here? I must go out and take care of my baby." She swam to the surface, reached the shore, and walked toward Jung-Ja and me. She doesn't remember anything after that. She passed out and fell on the ground. Jung-Ja ran to her and pulled her close to the fire to warm her up. When Mom came to, she felt extreme pain and realized that one side of her body was burned because she was too close to the fire. She didn't care about her pain; she picked me up and gave me her breast milk and sang a calming song for me. I stopped crying. As soon as Mom had her strength back, we walked back home.

Weeks after I was born—Mom was not sure exactly when—I developed a fever. Mom knew she should have taken me to the doctor, but she had no money. That time, because of the fever, Mom did not take me with her when she went diving. She left me home in the care of Jung-Ja. Jung-Ja told me I cried all the time when Mom was not with me.

All Jung-Ja could do was watch me, clean me, and cover her ears to block my loud, constant crying. "What will happen to the baby?" Jung-Ja asked Mom every day. "If she lives, she lives; if she dies, she dies," Mom replied. "I cannot help her more; I have to think of the others too."

Jung-Ja thought I had cried for three days straight. I only stopped when Mom came home to feed me. The fever continued. I cried, I ate, and I barely slept. After three days, the fever stopped and so did my constant crying, Mom remembered. She could not believe I had survived on my own. She believed I was here to stay and held me in her arms.

Chapter 3

"Do You Want Me to Tell You About My Mom?"

Mom was born in Koje Do in 1916 and she had four brothers and two sisters. She was very pretty. She was tall for a Korean woman at that time—about 5' 4"—like I am now. She was thin and had long, straight black hair and brown eyes. She was so pretty when she was a teenager that boys could not stop looking at her. This made her four brothers uneasy. They were very protective of her. They told her to walk looking down, not up. If she looked up and talked to people in the streets, her brothers became upset and gave her a hard time. They scolded her and insisted that she did not ever raise her eyes when she was walking in the street. "Don't look up! You are too pretty!" they demanded.

Mom got married when she was nineteen years old. She followed the tradition of the time. Her marriage was arranged between her parents and her husband-to-be's parents. She had no other option; her parents would pick a husband for her and she would marry him. Mom never saw her husband before the wedding. Nobody told her if he was short or tall, thin or fat, or if he had a mild or strong personality. Nobody told her what he did for a living, what he liked or disliked, or the sound of his voice. She didn't know anything about him, and she didn't dare ask. If she had asked her parents, they would have replied that she did not need to worry about the type of man she was going to marry. Her parents would make the choice and her duty as a daughter was to accept their choice without hesitation. This was very hard for Mom to accept, but she did.

Nevertheless, she worried about her future husband. She wondered about his appearance. What if he's missing an ear? Or a finger? Mom worried about this all the time. After waiting for what seemed like endless months, the wedding day arrived. Mom dressed simply. I don't know the exact details of her dress. It must have been a simple, traditional Korean wedding of the time.

Mom was extremely nervous on her wedding day. Not only was she going to be married, she was finally going to meet her husband. She would have the chance to look at Dad. Was he handsome? She couldn't answer her questions right away. Mom had to look down during the whole ceremony. She could not look at her husband-to-be. She wanted to, but the stern look of her brothers made her think twice before raising her eyes to get even a glimpse of the man she was going to marry. Does he fulfill her expectations of a handsome husband? She had to wait a bit longer to know the answer.

After the wedding ceremony, the newlyweds, their parents, and their guests celebrated in a party room. Mom and Dad sat at a small and short Korean-style table in the center of the room. On the table, there was rice, kimchi, and Makeli wine, which is a traditional Korean rice wine from the countryside. They also had other foods to enjoy during their first meal as husband and wife. Their table was decorated with two traditional wooden ducks, which symbolize fidelity and a long life together as a couple, just as some ducks remain coupled in nature.

After they had enjoyed their meal with their family and gone to

Wedding ducks.

their private room, Mom decided that she was not going to wait any longer to meet her husband. She looked directly at Dad's face, directly into his eyes. Mom's mouth opened and her eyes widened. He was very handsome! "You are a very good looking man!" she exclaimed. But right away her surprise vanished. She frowned and thought, hmm, he is good looking, but maybe he walks with a limp. She asked Dad, "Can you stand up and walk?"

Dad looked at her, amazed, and replied, "Why are you asking me this?"

"I am only worried about my husband. What if there is something wrong? I don't have a choice. My parents arranged my marriage, but I am still worried about my husband. I just want to see if everything is fine. I need to know!"

"OK," Dad said. He stood up and walked around the room in long, smooth steps, looking up and ahead. "Is this OK now?" he asked. "I have never heard of this before, of a woman asking her husband to stand and walk around the room on the honeymoon night."

It was true. All women look down, even on the honeymoon night, but Mom did not. She looked directly at Dad's eyes and told him to walk. She was pleased with what she had seen so far. Dad was a handsome man, he had both ears, and he didn't walk with a limp. Now she had another type of question for Dad.

"When a woman and man get married, who is the boss?" Mom asked him. "I am strong. I can tell you what to do and you would listen and do what I say."

"That's not true," Dad said, lowering his voice.

"But it is," Mom replied.

"We'll see."

That was their first conversation as a married couple. It was a very unusual conversation for any marriage in any part of the world, but Mom was an unusual woman. Her strength and determination would become very useful later in her life.

Mom and Dad spent their wedding night in a small two-room house in the village, close to her parent's home. The wood-framed sliding doors covered with rice paper were perfect to fulfill the wedding night tradition. According to the tradition, a few of the people living in the village had to quietly approach the house when Mom and Dad were spending their first honeymoon night together. The neighbors would wet one finger and make a hole on the rice paper covering the door and look inside. Has the marriage been consummated? Somebody had to check! If the wedding night was not successful, tradition promised that a tiger would descend from the mountain and attack the villagers. The tiger didn't come that night.

For about a year Mom and Dad lived happily in Koje Do. They had their own home. It was small but very nice. It was a traditional Korean home, like others in the village, made of wood with a thatched roof. Their home rested on a base above the ground with a space between the base and the house's floor. In the winter, Mom and Dad placed glowing coals in this space to warm up the floor on which they slept. They slept over blankets and a thin mat, the typical Korean bed. Their home had two rooms—one for cooking and eating and one for sleeping. Wood-framed sliding doors covered with rice paper provided some privacy.

Mom dove often and collected enough abalone, octopus, seaweed, and other sea foods to sell and for them to eat. Dad also had a job at that time. I don't remember what it was, but for about a year after they got married, they enjoyed a struggle-free life. They did not have expensive clothes nor live in a large house, but both had jobs and earned enough to have all their basic needs covered. In time, however, things changed for the worse for my parents.

During my parents' life, Korea was going through very tough times. In 1910, Japan annexed Korea to its territory (Dad was born in 1909 or 1908, I am not quite sure, and Mom in 1916) and the Japanese army was permanently present in Korean land to enforce Japanese ruling.

Throughout the subsequent years, life for the majority of Korean families changed for the worse. In my family, the Japanese government confiscated all of my paternal grandparents' properties; they lost all they had. Some families, my Mom and Dad included, had to leave Korea for Japan at one time or another, looking for better job opportunities. My two oldest brothers and two oldest sisters were born in Japan, and although our parents were Korean, they received Japanese names, according to the law at the time. Years later, when my family returned to Korea, my siblings changed their Japanese names back to their Korean names, just like all other Koreans in their situation did.

My parents got married in 1935. Four years later, World War II began and by 1941 Japan had actively joined the war after the attack on Pearl Harbor. Japan's involvement in World War II made Korea's internal situation even more stressful. My parents lived through a time when Korea and Japan suffered tremendous instability and this dramatically affected my parents' lives, their choices, and their future.

When Mom told me that she once had confronted armed Japanese soldiers, I was convinced that she could do anything. My parents were returning by boat to Koje Do after traveling to another village to buy rice. At the time, there were armed Japanese soldiers almost everywhere in Korea. They were in the roads between villages and towns, in city streets, in docks, and in any traveling routes used by Koreans. Surveillance was constant and usually the Japanese soldiers took whatever they thought was of any value from Koreans. In this case, it was a sack of rice.

Mom and Dad were disembarking from the boat when a Japanese soldier stopped Dad at the edge of the dock. Dad was carrying a big sack of rice over his shoulder and this had caught the attention of the Japanese soldier.

"Give me that rice!" the soldier demanded.

"No, I need to take it home to feed my family," Dad replied, his eyes looking down to the ground.

"If you don't give me the rice…," said the soldier, raising his voice. He lifted the rifle he was carrying over one shoulder with both hands and threw a blow at Dad's shoulder, trying to hit him with the rifle's butt. But he missed! Dad had moved fast to one side, avoiding the strike. The soldier hit the air and almost lost his balance. This made him very angry.

The soldier tried to kick Dad, but again, Dad dodged the strike and the soldier missed. The soldier raised his rifle and pointed at Dad, almost point blank. "Give. Me. The. Rice," he repeated, very slowly.

Mom jumped in front of Dad. "Shoot me first!" she demanded. "You cannot shoot my husband!"

"If you don't move," said the soldier keeping his aim at Mom, "I'll shoot you."

"You shoot me first, and then you shoot my husband," Mom replied, standing tall in front of Dad with her arms opened wide, facing the soldier. Dad was deathly still, the sack of rice firmly on his shoulder.

A high-ranking officer had heard the commotion and approached them. "Don't shoot the woman!" he ordered. He told the soldier to lower his rifle. "Aren't you afraid?" he asked Mom calmly, both his hands interlaced on his back.

"I cannot see the soldier shoot my husband; you have to shoot me first," she told the officer.

"You are a very brave woman," the officer said, amused. "You may go." He smiled and said, talking to himself, "Korea has very strong women."

Mom took the sack of rice from Dad's shoulder, swung it onto the top of her head and, pulling Dad by his belt, she said, "Let's go home."

One day Dad did not have a job in Korea anymore. He found one in Japan working in a shipyard that built fishing ships. They decided to move there, expecting to improve their economic situation. From the moment my parents moved to Japan, Mom felt that every day was a test to her physical strength and strong character. One of her toughest tests occurred when she was giving birth to my second oldest brother Hwa-Nam; it was towards the end of World War II.

The time had come for the baby to be born and Mom was resting on the floor of their small home with her back on a thin, faded blanket. She was trying to synchronize her breathing with the contractions when the sirens announcing an airborne attack went off. It was a very dark night. All the houses in the village had their windows covered with a dark cloth to conceal the house lights from airplane pilots flying above them, ready to drop their bombs as soon as they spotted a target.

The menacing roar of the American bomber plane engines grew louder and the contractions became more frequent. Mom told me that she could feel the baby making his way out. She had to breathe in unison with the contractions. She was sweating profusely, and she tried to ignore the soaring airplanes and the sirens. Soon, she hoped, it would be over and they could leave the house for a better refuge. Just a bit longer. . . The sirens, her screams, the roaring airplanes, and suddenly everybody beside her—my Dad and my two older sisters—ran away. They left the house and her inside of it, all by herself in the middle of the delivery.

"Oh, no, no," Mom said, realizing she was alone. "What did you do?" I asked her. "What could I do?" she replied. "I had no choice but to stay and take care of the baby being born right there and then in the middle of a bomber attack. That's the only thing that mattered in that moment."

My brother was born and Mom took care of herself and the baby. She had no clean sheets or soft blankets to wrap the tiny baby boy with, so she used the old, ragged, and stained, thin blanket Mom was resting on to clean and cover the baby's tiny body. She did not have scissors or a knife to cut the umbilical cord with, so she cut it with her teeth. She stayed in the house for a while. The airplanes left without causing any harm to the village. When the noises calmed down, Mom got up and found water to clean the baby and herself. She moved on with the usual routines as if nothing had happened. That's who she was. For her, panic was a useless feeling that just got in the way of getting the right thing done.

During the time my parents lived in Japan, my oldest brother passed away when he was a baby. This made Mom and Dad very sad. Mom was so upset with herself for not being able to save her son that when she returned to Koje Do a few years later, she decided to do something about it. She sought out the village healer, an old grandmother, and learned some traditional emergency healing techniques and she used them with her other children and any others who might need them. Sometimes she helped children alleviate a stomach ache by using simple acupuncture techniques. During her life, she successfully treated hundreds of babies that might otherwise have suffered or even died. She never charged money for this, but the babies' parents always gave her rice, fruit, or some other necessity even though she never asked for anything. She said that she remembered all too well how she felt when she could not save her baby and didn't want others to feel that kind of pain.

Return to Korea

When World War II ended in 1945 and Korea was no longer annexed by Japan, my parents decided to go back home. Dad found passage for my family in a small ship that carried only ten people. They packed and loaded all their belongings in the ship and Mom; my brother Hwa-Nam, who was only a baby; my sisters, Choon-Ja and Jung-Ja; and Dad boarded the ship on a sunny morning with a calm sea.

Half way through their journey, the weather changed. A storm developed quickly, blowing tremendous gales and causing high waves. The small ship swung side to side precariously, up and down with the waves. The women were crying; the children were screaming and holding tight to their mothers' clothes and bodies. Mom had my brother in her arms and my two sisters held onto her clothes desperately. One of my sisters, Choon-Ja, was feeling more seasick by the minute, until she cried, "Mom, I feel like I am going to throw up!"

Mom was overwhelmed by the threatening storm, the balancing boat, and afraid for the lives of her family. "Then throw up!" she replied to my sister's cry.

"Where?"

"Wherever you want to!"

Mom was sitting on a box and Choon-Ja was standing on the box, hugging her with both arms around Mom's neck. Choon-Ja could not hold it any longer; she threw up on Mom's head. I laughed when Mom told me this story, but she felt disgusted recalling the long-past memory. She still remembered it vividly, like it had just happened.

The storm almost made the boat capsize a few times. The captain was afraid people might need to jump ship to save their lives, but when he gave the order to jump, Mom protested angrily.

"We live or die together," she cried. "I know how to swim, but my children don't." She reached for a rope on the deck and tied her children and herself together. "I won't jump. If you want us to leave the boat, you have to throw us over board together."

Dad and the ship captain looked at her with a mixture of admiration and puzzlement, then they looked at each other. She must have been some sight: wet, angry, and with vomit dripping down from her head. They decided not to argue with her. The captain gave orders to throw overboard all the belongings people had brought with them. Making the ship lighter helped it stay afloat during the storm, but my family was left with nothing to bring back home; they only had each other. Mom hung on to her children, and in time the storm calmed down and the boat made it to Korean shores safely.

They arrived on the mainland dripping wet, seasick, and scared. They had lost everything they had brought back home to start a new life. They landed in Korea with nothing. They had no money, no clothes, no utensils, no furniture, nothing. Going back home turned out to be much harder than they had anticipated. They traveled back to Koje Do and lived with Mom's family for a while.

Once again, Mom used her diving expertise to bring money home. There were many other haenyo like Mom trying to make a living from harvesting what the sea provided, but this was not a problem. Sea food was abundant in Koje Do; there was plenty for all the people in the village. Sometimes, a group of haenyo dove together.

Mom expanded her seafood sales, adding other products she brought from the mainland to sell in Koje Do. She had a good mind for business and she was successful. Her earnings increased and she had more than enough to feed the family and provide for all other needs. She had extra money to save and later on she bought a little house. In a few years, they moved from my grandparents' home to their own modest, two-room home in Koje Do. Mom was almost completely happy.

Things went well for a while until Dad took a wrong turn with his life. He went back to his old habits and did not help Mom take care of family responsibilities. He did not help her with anything. This already made things more difficult for Mom, who now had four children to take care of. The situation took a turn for the worse when Dad took money from Mom's savings to gamble and lost it all.

Mom hid the money from him, but he insisted so much that she give it to him, deciding to do as he asked to avoid more violent confrontations. When Mom told me about this, her eyes watered and she became very quiet for a while. What could she do? He did not understand reason. He became demanding and impatient. The situation slowly grew out of hand. Mom felt trapped. Korean tradition forbade her to leave her husband; she had to take care of him, even when he was not contributing to provide for their home's needs. Even when he was making things worse for her and the children, she had to care for him. It must have been a very difficult time. I try to put myself in her place, and I am not sure I would have been as patient as she was.

"What happened to Dad?" I asked.

Mom looked at me with swollen eyes and whispered. "I think something was really wrong in his mind," she said. "I think he lost it."

Mom thought that because he never had to work for food and shelter, he never learned to assume responsibilities; he evaded them when he was younger and he was doing the same now. And when it was time to face the situation and work, he did not know what to do. Mom, on the other hand, had learned to work to meet her family's needs when she was young. It was obvious to her that working was the means to sustaining the family.

The Korean War, which began in 1950, brought more strenuous times and a hopeless future for many Koreans. Some of them, like Dad, could not cope with it and gave up. He did not care for our family or himself. He just wanted to ease the depression and frustrations of living in a country with very limited opportunities by gambling and drinking and taking it out on Mom and his children. After the Korean War ended in 1953, it took decades for the country and the people to recover and live more prosperous lives.

Mom was different. Her children were her first priority, and she would go hungry for days so her children could eat. She would sew clothes for us at night when we were sleeping using an oil lamp with a wick that barely provided any light. We had no electricity in Koje Do and candles were expensive.

Many neighbors who were aware of the situation at home told Mom to leave Dad, give my brothers and sisters up for adoption, and leave Koje Do for another place with more possibilities. "Start over again on your own," they advised her. But Mom said she could never do it. She would not abandon her children, just as she had not abandoned them when the storm almost capsized the boat taking them back to Korea. Mom swallowed all her pride, anger, and frustration. She did not let depression get the best of her and continued working hard and sometimes hopelessly to keep the family alive and together. This was the world I was born into. I understand now why it was hard for my mom and dad to welcome me.

The first six years of my life are like a blur in my mind. I remember little things here and there, but for the most part my memories are confusing and uncertain. However, I have specific memories of things that happened to me and my family that have been preserved clearly in my mind.

Easier to remember, though, are my feelings in those times. I really hated how I lived as a child. I remember vividly the feeling of constant hunger. My brothers and sisters, Mom, and I sometimes went to bed after having just a few vegetables for dinner. I remember having potatoes and corn many times, but sometimes nothing. Rice was expensive for us, so we rarely ate it. We usually had a small bowl of rice on special occasions, such as a birthday party or New Year's celebration. I think this is the reason I value rice so much now. I wanted to eat it when I was a little girl, but I couldn't. It was almost a delicacy, like caviar or another special food you have only on certain occasions. We were hungry most of the time.

I vividly remember being cold, very cold. Winter in Koje Do was long and hard. The freezing, humid breeze from the ocean permeated through our bones and at night we huddled into each other on the floor, trying to keep our bodies warm. We did not have money to buy enough coal to heat the floor of the house from below. Any little amount of coal we placed there quickly lost its heat in the freezing and windy Koje Do winter.

Mom placed a few little bowls with water beside our heads before we went to sleep, just in case we were thirsty in the middle of the night. I remember the water in the bowls was frozen solid when we woke up in the morning. I was glad that we had each other to keep warm and did not freeze like the water.

I have never forgotten the feeling of helplessness, of being in a situation I did not like at all and not being able to do anything about it. I remember not being able to warm my body with layers of clothes or a thick coat. I remember not having enough coal or even pieces of wood to light a fire to warm me up. I remember not knowing what to do to end the painful turning of my stomach and its emptiness. Being helpless to change my bad situation is the worst feeling I have ever had. I did not want to live like that anymore. I did not want my children to live like that ever. At that time, my way out of desperation was using my fertile imagination to daydream my way out of misery. I imagined what I wanted my life to be like at that time and in the future.

I walked on the beach in front of my house, shoeless and covered with a hand-me-down jacket over my skinny body. My only solace was my dog, Nabi, an energetic companion about the size and color of a yellow Labrador retriever that walked with me on the beach. As we walked slowly, I poked the soft sand. I poked it, and poked it with a thin stick with a sharp point. I was looking for crabs to eat and also daydreaming about what type of clothes I would like to wear to keep me warm in the winter. I would like a thick jacket, new, not a hand-me-down, colorful and long—almost to my feet to keep the wind away. I would like Mom to be around more often and to be able to cook for us every day, so we could have our bellies full and our bodies warm and satisfied from the inside. I dreamed of having a big bowl of steaming rice in front of me at the table, together with a variety of fish and vegetables and seaweed. I would drink hot tea and Mom would have rice wine, which would also warm her up. We would have enough money to buy plenty of coal in the winter to keep the house warm, and the water by our heads would not freeze. I would have warm and soft new shoes; I might even have a thick beret warming up my head and ears. I hated my cold, hungry, hopeless life and told myself I did not want my children to live like this. But, what could I do?

I could not do much then to make my life better; not even close to my dream, but I promised myself that things would be different when I grew up. I would find a way to reach my dream. I would find a way to fulfill my needs. I was a little girl, walking on the beach, poking holes in the wet sand and repeating to myself that, one day, I would have a warm home, warm clothes, and a better life, far away from my misery.

I was only six or seven years old, but I often thought about how we lived, and how we merely survived. It was true that we were hungry, cold, and miserable most of the time. But I realized that in spite of all our problems, my brothers and sisters and I were together. We had stayed together no matter what. We had a family. We had not been abandoned, like other kids had been by their parents—which neighbors had recommended my Mom do to free herself from the burden of children. We stayed together. Most importantly, we had someone to look up to. We had someone to turn to, even though most of the time there was not much she could do. We had Mom. I was seven, but I could see all this.

Mom was not around the house very often. I spent most of the days by myself, but I know she wasn't around because she was looking for food, coal, wood, or anything that would help us make it through the day. Mom held us together; she had not given up on us.

She had not given up on me, the last one to join the family in bad times. It is true she tried to stop the pregnancy, but when she realized that nothing she tried had worked to stop me, she accepted me. I was thankful that she had not thrown me into the ocean right after I was born, which other desperate mothers had done with their babies. I was thankful she had prevented Dad from throwing me into the ocean.

She did not take me to the doctor when I had a fever for days, but she came home often to feed me, hold me, and hug me, and had my sister watch me in her absence. She did not give up on me. I think she did the best she could under the extreme circumstances of her life, overwhelmed as she was with so many insurmountable responsibilities. She kept us children together; we were not on our own. We had Mom. I could not get out of my situation on my own, but it struck me then that there was something I could do. I could help Mom, as best as I could, to ease her load. She was holding us together. I had to do my part.

I had a plan. From that day on, when Mom went to work in the morning, I would climb the mountain behind my home with Nabi. My dog usually came with me when I climbed the mountain; I was sure he would love to accompany me every morning. In the mountain, I would do what I had seen Mom do many times before when she had not been successful finding food of any kind anywhere else. I would climb the ragged mountain, holding on to boulders and shrubs, and would pull out any edible plant, shrub, or root. Back at home, I would rinse and scrub the plants I had collected and cook them in a pot filled with boiling water for an hour or two. Mom said, "Until soft, so we don't have to chew on hard pieces." We would have soup for dinner.

In the mountain, I would also collect pieces of wood, tree bark, or other plant materials good for making a fire. Mom made a fire daily for cooking and to keep us warm. These two things I could do to help Mom. I was skinny, but strong and committed to this mission. Mom did not tell me to do it, but I knew I had to help her.

Chapter 4

The Octopus in the Cave

The day I fed the whole village—well, almost the whole village—had started as a very boring day, but it ended with a beach party. I think I was about seven or eight years old. I was by myself, as usual, after Mom had left home to look for food or a job. None of my brothers or my sisters were at home. After I had climbed the mountain and collected a few plants and wood, I had nothing else to do.

I stepped outside, facing the beach, but the view was as lonely outside as it was inside the house. The beach was deserted and only a few elderly people remained in the village. The majority of the adults and young people had gone to school or to find work wherever they could get it. I left the house holding my long, thin stick in hand and strolled along the solitary beach.

I reached a place I had seen before, but I had never explored it. It was a small cave that had an entrance right where the waves reached the shore. Three or more huge boulders much taller and wider than me leaned on each other, supporting their own weight, like enormous domino pieces resting on each other, standing on their shorter sides. The oddly stacked rocks formed an opening among them—a natural, small cave.

At night the sea poured into the cave, covering the rocks to about half of their height. By day, the sea receded, leaving only small puddles of seawater trapped in sand pits among small rocks lying on the ground. I looked at the cave from a distance. There was not much water inside at the moment; it looked safe to explore. I decided to go inside.

It was dark and cold inside the cave. I had just walked a couple of steps inside when I heard an unusual sound mixed with the lapping of the waves. The deep sound was like the noise made by someone breathing very deeply and heavily. Was there someone trapped inside? I couldn't see very well; my eyes were still getting used to the dim light inside the cave. I walked further in, taking small, slow steps, guiding my way with my stick. As my eyes adjusted. I began to see more clearly. Then I saw it.

An enormous octopus was lying flat on the sandy cave bottom, barely covered by seawater. The octopus was as big as a three-seat couch! One of its arms, lined with suckers the size of my fist, was nearly a foot thick. I immediately knew what had happened to the poor octopus. The high tide at night had brought this giant creature—this giant meal for the village—inside the cave. But when the tide receded in the morning, the octopus had been trapped. Now, with barely enough water to cover its huge, thick body, the magnificent creature had no means to breathe or to escape to safer, deeper water. It was having a hard time catching enough air from the shallow puddles that surrounded it; it was dying, trapped in the cave.

The thought came to me right away. Wouldn't it be a very good thing if I could bring the octopus home to eat? We wouldn't be hungry for many days. Mom would not have to worry about food for a while.

Using my stick, I poked the octopus several times but it didn't move at all. I slid my stick through the band around my waist; I needed both my hands free if I was going to hoist this monster meal home. Each octopus arm was bigger than my torso. I grabbed one of its thick arms with both hands and pulled, but nothing happened. It was quite slippery, so I cleaned my hands on my shirt and tried again. I pulled and pulled, again to no avail. The big monster was too heavy for me to pull it out of the cave alone. I was going to need help. I ran back to the village looking for people who could give me a hand.

At first, the only people I could find were very sick or too old. I could not ask them to help me in any way. I ran along the beach, hoping to find at least one person strong enough to help me carry the octopus to the village. There, far down the beach, I found a teenaged friend who had not left home yet. I ran toward him and pleaded, "You need to follow me, please! I want to show you this very big octopus!"

He was not interested in my cries. "Go home; don't bother me!" he yelled back at me.

I was not going to give up that easily. He was the only person I could find that looked strong enough to help me.

I insisted, "No, no, you need to come!" I grabbed his arm with both my hands and tried to pull him toward the cave. I needed to make him understand how important this was for the whole village. "I have found a giant octopus trapped in a cave. You have to help me bring it to the village. Can you imagine having more food than you can possibly eat at once?" It finally worked; I had persuaded him to go to the cave so he could see it with his own eyes.

When he saw the amazing octopus, he gawked and placed both hands over his forehead. He tried to pull the octopus out of the cave as I had tried before, but he couldn't. It was too heavy, even with both of us pulling together. Without saying a word, he ran back to the village, found a few of his friends, and ran back to the cave where I was waiting, watching the octopus. It was breathing slower and shallower by the minute.

Four young men finally managed to carry the octopus in one piece out of the cave and to the beach. It was not breathing anymore. By then, many people from the village had returned home, gathering and chattering around the huge creature resting on the sand.

They began to clean, cut, and divide the octopus. I just sat back and watched in amazement and anger. I was the one who had found the octopus! No one thanked me or congratulated me. I was completely overlooked and ignored. On top of that, all the pieces were being divided between the people on the beach, but nobody gave a piece to me.

I wanted to show Mom the huge octopus I had found, but how could I do that when it was being cleaned and cut up into smaller pieces right in front of my eyes? I was really upset, but nevertheless I told myself that it would be OK. Mom would not come back from work until late in the evening and the entire village could not wait for Mom to come home from work to start cleaning and cooking this octopus. With that in mind, I pushed my anger aside and tried to help cook the octopus. It was so big that everybody in the village would have a share of the catch.

We had a big beach party that night. We made a few big fires on the beach and placed large pots on top, in which we cooked the octopus after cutting it into many pieces. Everybody living in the village was at the party eating octopus, but Mom and the rest of my family were not there yet. I had to make sure we would get our fair share.

"Sir, I found this octopus!" I told a man cooking in one of the pots. "My Mom and my family aren't here to eat with us yet."

"Here, take this home!" he said. And he gave me an enormous octopus arm. It felt like it weighed a ton. I nodded, thanking him. I swung the long octopus arm over my shoulder and slowly dragged it home. I was so happy that I had found this giant octopus. With a smile on my face, I walked home as tall as I could under the heavy weight of the animal's arm that would feed us for many days. Actually, as I realized later, I had not thought much about the implications of receiving a big octopus arm as a reward.

When I arrived home, Mom was already there. She heard me calling her name and when she opened the door, her eyes widened in shock. I expected Mom to look thrilled at this huge octopus arm our family was going to feast on, and I imagined she would calmly put on her outside shoes and walk over to help me with this leg. I was so wrong.

As soon as she snapped out of her shock, she ran out the door barefoot, which was very strange because she never walked outside without shoes. I gave her the octopus arm and she placed it on the ground. She turned to me and demanded to know where this octopus arm came from and whose it was. I explained my entire octopus adventure, describing my exploration of the rocks and the discovery of the octopus all the way to the beach party. I told her I was upset that I never had the chance to show her the whole octopus. "It was my octopus, Mom! I found it and they just started cleaning it and cooking it and when I tried to tell them I found it and that I wanted to show it to you, they only gave me this arm to bring home," I said.

Mom looked very angry, but I didn't know why. She took my hand and said we were going to visit the beach party. Once we arrived there, she scolded everyone. "This is Choon-Ok's octopus! Everybody needs to thank my daughter for finding and sharing this octopus right now," she told everybody. People turned away from the cooking pots and looked at her. They knew she was someone worth paying attention to. They looked at me and thanked me, bowing to me lightly, and after everyone had thanked me, Mom and I joined the party. We all joked around and had a good time, Mom especially. She would jokingly say, "My daughter found this octopus. How come she only got one arm?"

"Well, if we gave her two arms she couldn't carry them home!" said a friend with a laugh. Mom seemed pleased after everybody had thanked me and appreciated that I had shared the whole octopus I had found with everybody in the village.

In the following days, I came to realize that the reward for finding the octopus had unexpected consequences. On each of the next ten days, I had octopus for breakfast, lunch, and dinner from that one arm. It was always the same food, three meals every day. I grew sick and tired of eating octopus, but I knew better than to complain about this, until one day I could not stay quiet anymore.

"Mom, I don't want octopus anymore!"

She laughed. "Well, what else are you going to eat then? If you don't want to eat octopus, then don't eat it," she said. We knew there was no other food in the house besides the octopus, so I apologized and reluctantly asked for more.

When I told this story to my daughters, Emerald and Jada, they paid close attention to it. They were amazed and also amused at the irony of my story.

"I can't believe you ate the same thing for every meal, ten days in a row!" they said.

Hearing my octopus story also raised their interest in my childhood home in Koje Do.

They asked questions about the beach I walked back and forth on every day, poking the sand with my stick, looking for little crabs to eat. They asked questions about the cave where I discovered the octopus. Did I find any more octopi in the cave later on? Unfortunately—or fortunately, depending on how you look at it—I only found one octopus in all my years in Koje Do. My daughters also became interested in the home I lived in when I was a little girl, with a mountain out back I could climb any time I wanted to, and a beach out front where I would never go swimming. All these places were very different from the urban setting my daughters were used to in the suburbs of a modern American city like Houston, Texas.

We began to talk often about the places of my childhood in Koje Do, and one day, my husband and I decided that in our next trip to Korea we would visit Koje Do with our daughters. We would show them the little house where I grew up, the cave that trapped the giant octopus, and the long, sandy beach on which I had created my dream.

In 2002, my husband, my two daughters, and I traveled to Koje Do. For me, this trip would be like traveling back in time and reliving the experiences of my childhood. We all had great expectations and were excited. Maybe this is the reason I ended up more disappointed than happy after going back.

The village I saw when we arrived was very different from the one I remembered. The beach of my childhood and the octopus cave had disappeared. They now existed only in my childhood memories. Instead of an open, wide beach, there were many docks lined up with big boats, small boats, and fishing boats. I would not be able to run from home to the beach any more, as I had done countless times when I was a little girl. Now, I could only run along the docks and between the boats.

The octopus cave had been reduced to a few small boulders. The huge rocky blocks that leaned on each other like domino pieces had been cut into smaller pieces and used for construction, probably for the docks that now sat on the beach. I could not show my daughters the beach I remembered or the cave where the octopus had been trapped by the tide. I wondered what else was gone.

We walked slowly toward the place where my home used to be. My home was not there anymore, either. My childhood home had been replaced with a small grocery store to supply the needs of the local residents. My eyes filled with tears. What else had vanished?

I walked behind the store and saw that the mountain was still there. Of course I did not expect a mountain to vanish in just a few decades, but the mountain actually looked much smaller than I remembered it. I guess I grew up and the mountain didn't.

I told my daughters about my good times on the mountain in the

Choon-Ok, Barry, Emerald, and Jada in Koje Do, 2002. The house behind them stands where Choon-Ok's childhood home used to be.

company of my brother Choon-Duk. I loved to follow him and do what he liked to do; Mom said I was a tomboy. Choon-Duk always asked Mom, "Tell her not to follow me everywhere!" I did not like to play with dolls or other girl games; I loved to do what boys liked to do. I ran up and down the mountain; I climbed trees and swung on their branches. My brother taught me how to make my own own sling shot. We caught birds with the sling shot and cooked them over a campfire. Choon-Duk had a net and he fished in the ocean with it. We cleaned the fish using a knife and ate fresh fish right away, sushi-sashimi style. Everything we caught, we ate. Nothing went to waste.

I asked some of the people now living in the village about the changes I saw in the mountain. They told me that rocks and dirt had been removed from the mountain and used for construction over the years, eventually reducing its size. People might not be able to move a mountain, but they can erode it down to nothing in time, very much like water and wind can.

My childhood home was no longer as I remembered. It had been changed to something different, reduced in size, or simply erased. I did not like the changes I saw. I liked it much better the way it looked when I was a little girl. I was sad that I could not show my daughters my childhood home, the beach, the mountain, and the octopus cave. They could only see how the same areas look in the present. How these places looked in the past is stored in my memory, and they will stay alive somehow in this memoir.

Remembering the Past

As we walked along the docks built where my beach used to be, other images and feelings rushed back into my memory, and I told my daughters about them. The first memory that I recalled was of the time when I became afraid of water. "It was around here, I think, when it happened," I told them, pointing at the water and looking back and around to orient myself in this place.

I was six or seven years old and my brother Choon-Duk and I were playing in the shallow waters of the beach. We were chasing each other. I was trying to catch Choon-Duk and push him into the water, but he began to swim toward deeper water, attempting to escape from my pursuit. I did not know how to swim, so I continued chasing him, running through the water and jumping over small waves, reaching forward with my arms, when unexpectedly I sank into deep water. All of a sudden, the seafloor disappeared from under my feet and I dropped several feet, the water high over my head. I panicked.

I did not know how to handle the situation. I didn't know how to swim. How can I describe the terror and helplessness I felt as I began to drown? There was nothing my hands could hold on to, nothing my feet could kick off from. Seawater filled my mouth as my lungs screamed for air, but there was no air and I was paralyzed with fear. I didn't want to die. I kicked hard. I slapped the water as hard as I could in an attempt to keep my head above the water, but I kept sinking. I don't know how long this situation lasted, but it felt like a very long time until Choon-Duk pulled me out and carried me toward the beach. He laid me down on the sand and pushed my stomach with both hands. I coughed and vomited up the seawater I had swallowed. I could breathe now. I was not going to die.

I cried and cried, and later that evening I told my mom, "I never want to go to that place again!" She just rubbed my back and hugged me and I felt safe. From that time forth, I did not like the water and I did not enjoy going in the sea at all.

I put the issue of swimming out of my mind for many years. I thought that as long I stayed away from deep water and did not venture into situations that brought me close to deep water, I did not have to worry. This reasoning worked well for me for years until I had my children.

After I had my first daughter, Emerald, I told myself that I needed to learn to swim. What if something happened to my daughter like it had happened to me in the sea? I had to be able to swim to help her from drowning, like my brother had saved me years ago.

Here I was, reliving in my mind one of the memories that had scared me the most. It seemed that I would have to fight and defeat this fear and learn to swim. What if I didn't learn? I imagined my young daughters walking around our pool and accidentally falling in it. I know the fear they would feel trying to reach the edge of the pool or a shallow area, unsuccessfully kicking and splashing the water with their arms. I could not stand this terrible thought. I would learn to swim and my daughters would learn too. I pushed myself to forget about my fear and I learned to float and swim in deep water. I had to do it.

I have a fond memory of the time I learned to float and swim. When I was learning to float on my back, I was very pregnant with my second daughter, Jada, and my stomach stuck out above the water. It looked very funny. My husband laughed hard, because he said that my stomach looked like a small watermelon. From that day on, he affectionately called Jada "my little watermelon."

Spending a few days in Koje Do revived many more memories and my daughters were delighted to hear them. We were walking away from the grocery store where my home used to be. We had the ocean on one side and houses and the worn-down mountain on the other. Ahead of us, the narrow dirt path snaked around the other mountains in the area until it reached the next village. My village is located in the area of Kom Po.

I remembered this dirt path very well, because I had walked it many times during the day with Mom or one of my siblings on our way to the next village to find food, a job, or to go to school. There was nothing but dirt; there was some vegetation and the sounds of animals would entertain us during the journey. There were many birds and there were snakes. The snakes occasionally crossed the road. Some snakes were so long that they could spread their bodies across the path, blocking our way as they slithered slowly from one side to the other.

One day, I was on the road walking to school on my own when I came across a very large snake. I froze instantly when I saw it. It was so big that I did not dare to walk over it. I did not even try to go around it. I had to wait. I had my stick with me and I pounded the ground around the snake with the stick in a futile attempt to encourage the snake to go faster. But there was no way I could make the thick, long, slow snake hurry across the road. Once it had crossed the road, I continued on my way.

I thought I knew the dirt path between the villages very well, but the neighbors told me that the road was different at night. It wasn't nearly as safe as it was during the day. It was pitch-black, unless you were lucky that night and the sky was clear and the moon was shining. There were robbers sometimes, and there were dangerous animals that roamed along the road, looking for something to eat. "Don't go out there at night," the neighbors warned me. It seemed like good advice. I wasn't worried about that though. We never went out at night. Or so I thought.

It happened when I was probably about nine years old. Mom, who never complained about body discomforts or pain, suddenly had trouble breathing deeply. She put her hands over her stomach and said, "I have something here." I touched her stomach with my hands and felt a lump moving up and down as she was breathing. Mom said that the lump was preventing her from breathing deeply. I could tell she was also in pain and was a little scared. She had had something like this before, usually after an argument with Dad that had upset her very much. On those occasions, the pain had dissipated when she drank a few sips of "Soju," a potato liquor that tastes like Vodka. The liquor seemed to diminish the pressure of the lump so she could breathe more easily.

We didn't have any liquor or wine in the house, of course; it was not on the top of the list of our basic needs, so Mom could not drink any at that time. The day moved on and Mom did not mention being short of breath anymore. We put it out of our minds. At night, though, things got worse—much worse.

We were sleeping when Mom screamed and woke us up in an instant. We felt confused and sleepy, but not for long. Mom continued screaming and in no time my brothers, sisters, and I were kneeling on the floor by her side. Her body was folded like a ball; she was holding her stomach with her hands and screaming so loudly we had to cover our ears with our hands. Dad was not home. It was up to us to help Mom.

Mom begged us to give her Soju to ease the pain, but we didn't have any. Someone had to go to the nearest village to get the Soju Mom needed to feel better. Our village didn't have any Soju; we had asked around earlier in the day and found nothing.

It was a very dark night, dimly lit by a sliver of the moon; walking to the closest village following the dirt path would be dangerous. Animals certainly would be in the area coming down from the mountain as they usually did at night. They could easily attack whoever dared be on the road. Who would go to get Soju for Mom?

I told my sister, "Go get Soju! You are older!"

"No, I am scared," she said. "I don't want to go."

Mom screamed more and more in pain.

I told my brother to go, but he was scared too.

Mom had trouble breathing.

I could not take it anymore. My concern for Mom was bigger than my fear of the animals that might stalk me on the dirt path. I sprinted through the door and ran as fast as I could through the dark, small path to the next village. When I arrived, most of the houses were dark; it was very late but I didn't care. I knocked on a couple of doors loudly, pleading to their kindness. "My Mom is dying! I need Soju to calm her pain!" I begged and cried until someone felt sorry for me and gave me a bit of Soju in a bottle. I held the bottle tight in one hand, said a quick thanks with a bow, and ran back home, focusing on not dropping the bottle on the hard ground.

Suddenly, I froze in my tracts. Right in front of me, only a few feet away, there were two little lights, one beside each other, maybe yellow or red, but I don't remember with certainty. They were very sharp and very bright. I knew they had to be the eyes of an animal standing in front of me, blocking my way back home and preventing me from delivering Soju to Mom. The unblinking eyes stared at me in silence, so I stared back. "I am stuck here, I cannot move," I thought. I was so scared. I opened the Soju bottle and took a couple of sips. I had drunk Soju before and did not like it. It tasted horrible. But that night I was so scared I noticed no taste at all; I only felt the warm liquid running down to my stomach.

I wasn't sure what type of animal it was; maybe it was similar to a coyote or a small wolf. Regardless of what animal I was facing, it was certainly dangerous. I was breathing fast, a combination of having been running and the fear I was facing at that moment. The creature was deadthly still. I was deathly still. We stared at each other for what felt like the longest ten minutes of my life; neither of us made a sound. I kept thinking, "If it attacks me, what will I do? I have this bottle in my hand; I could smack it with it." I was just waiting for its attack, ready to strike it with the bottle, when the animal slowly walked to the side of the road and the two tiny lights disappeared. In the silence of the night, I listened to the fading sound of its paws stepping on the ground until I could not hear them anymore. I ran home.

I arrived home with all my clothes soaked with sweat. Mom was still screaming and holding her abdomen. I knelt beside her and slowly placed the rim of the bottle to her lips, holding her head slightly up. She opened her lips a little and took a few sips, keeping her eyes closed. After a few sips more, she stopped screaming, calmed down, and fell asleep. Soju had done its job of relaxing Mom almost like magic, and I relaxed instantly too. I was so exhausted. I lay by her side and did not wake up until late the next morning.

When Mom woke up the next morning, the first thing she did was to ask, "Who brought Soju?"

"I did," I said.

"What about your brother and sister? They are older, why didn't they go instead of you?" She was getting upset.

"They didn't want to go," I explained.

Mom was now very angry at my brother and sister. She stood up slowly, supporting her body with both hands on the floor, as she carefully stood on one foot and then the other. She placed her hands on her hips and asked my brother and sister, "Did you tell her to go get Soju?"

"No, we did not tell her to go," whispered my brother and sister, looking at the floor and holding their hands behind their backs.

"Mom, nobody told me to go. I just ran on the dirt path to the next village to find Soju. You needed it so much to feel better," I explained.

"Never go again," she replied in a milder tone. "It's too dangerous."

"I know it's dangerous. I fought an animal in the dark road. I stared directly into its eyes for ten minutes. I did not move, I did not talk, just stared, and the animal did the same until he went away. I think I scared him," I said proudly.

Mom looked at me intensely, staring directly into my eyes. "Never go again. Don't do dangerous things. If Mom dies, it's fine, but you cannot die before I die," she said.

"I had to do it. I could not see you die!" was my response. I was about to cry, but did not want to.

Mom sat down on the floor and pulled my hand down, inviting me to sit with her. "Thank you," she said. "Of all your brothers and sisters you are the one I could not take care of. I could not give you enough food or even medicines when you needed them, and you always have hand-me-down clothes, but you went to get Soju for me."

"What do you mean, 'thank you'?" I replied. "Thank *you* for not throwing me into the ocean when I was a baby!" I laughed nervously.

"You have a lot of my personality," Mom said softly, looking me in the eye. "I never back down from a situation, and you don't seem to back down either. We are very much alike in temper and spirit. But if you never back down, you might get into trouble. You might get hurt sometimes. Be careful."

Mom cried quietly and left the house without another word. I waited inside the house, thinking about what she had said and what had happened. Mom returned soon with a piece of candy and gave it to me. "Thank you," she said.

Mom and I had important things in common, and I liked that because it brought us closer. However, I soon learned that sharing common ground did not mean we would never fight.

Chapter 5

No Money for School

I liked school. I liked to be with other children who were about my age and play, run, or climb trees. The days I spent in school flew by, which was just the opposite of the times I was all by myself at home. I also liked school because I loved to learn; I loved to know things. I still do.

I attended formal schooling for a while. It was a comforting break from my otherwise bleak day, when I was usually hungry, cold, or with nothing to do. At school I would forget about all those things. School was a place I loved to be.

I woke up early every morning to go to school. I had to walk for an hour before I reached the other side of the mountain in the area of Juh Gu Ri, where the school was located. At the end of my school day, I would retrace my steps and go back home. Everything was fine with this daily routine until one day the teacher asked me for the money.

At first, I did not understand what money she was talking about. When the teacher saw my puzzled face, she explained that parents needed to pay the school for their children's education. I told the teacher that I would ask Mom for money and headed back home. I retraced my steps very slowly that day. I already knew what Mom would say when I asked her for money to pay for school. I could almost hear her words: "There is no money for school."

On my way back home, I thought long and hard about how to convince Mom to pay for school. That would not be easy at all. When I arrived home, I waited for a while to ask for the money. I decided that it would be best to ask her when we were alone, sometime after dinner when she had finished with all the night's chores and my brothers and sisters were not around listening. I might have a better chance to strike a deal with her if we were alone and she was relaxed.

After an uneventful dinner, we picked up everything from the table, washed it, and put it away. Mom walked toward the back of the house and I followed her. She sat on a tree stump facing the mountain and smoked a cigarette to relax. I sat on the ground beside her and stirred the dirt in front of my feet with a small stick.

"I like school very much," I said, looking down at the dirt I had loosened with the stick. "I really like it."

"Good," Mom replied, blowing a cloud of smoke straight in front of her.

"The teacher asked me for money today," I said, almost whispering. "She said that everybody has to pay for schooling." I stopped stirring the dirt but continued looking down, waiting for Mom's reply.

Mom was about to bring the cigarette to her lips, but she paused for a second. She resumed her movement, released another cloud of smoke, and said, "I have no money for school."

I knew this was coming, so I appealed to her heart, which I knew had a special place for me. I began to cry softly. "I love school very much," I said between sobs. "I learn a lot and this is good for me, right?"

"I have no money for school," she repeated, raising her voice a bit. "Go anyway."

"But what will I tell the teacher when she asks for the money?" I looked up at her face. "I'd be so embarrassed to tell her we don't have it."

I was beginning to feel desperate. I pictured in my mind going to school the next day and spending the whole time trying to avoid my teacher. I would try to be out of her direct sight, sitting very still in the seat at the back of the room. I would keep the lowest profile possible during the whole day, but I was sure my teacher would see me sooner or later and then she would ask the dreaded question: "Choon-Ok, do you have the money for school?" All the kids would look at me, waiting for my answer. I told myself that I did not care about the other kids. But what if the teacher said that I could not come to school anymore until I brought the money? I did not want that to happen to me.

"Mom, I need the money for school!"

Mom dropped the cigarette butt on the ground. She stepped on it, grinding it with her shoe and then covering it with dirt. She stood up quickly. "No money, but you will go to school!"

I cried and cried, covering my face with both hands. I could feel Mom was losing her calm demeanor; she had her hands on her hips. She had said "no" several times already, but I wouldn't stop bothering her. Mom didn't like to tell us kids anything more than once. She felt that once was enough, and if she had to repeat herself it became a problem for us. Between my wet fingers I could see a frown forming on her forehead. "No money, but go to school," she repeated.

I was inconsolable; I could not stop crying. Mom looked to the right, then to the left, looking for something. Her eyes stopped at the corner of the house where a broom rested against the wall. She took a few quick steps toward the broom, grabbed it with both hands, and raised it against me. She was coming to hit me with the broom stick! I sprung to my feet in a fraction of a second, putting as much distance as possible between both of us, and avoiding the broom's reach. Mom did not stop her chase; on the contrary, she quickened her pace in my direction.

I ran toward the street, heading to the left side of the village and Mom ran behind me, holding the broom up with both hands. I did not stop running until I reached the last house in the village. Then I turned around, facing Mom, and let her get a little closer to me but not within the broom's reach. She slowed down her pace and swung the broom toward me. I faked right, but ran left, passing her in a dash. Mom did not give up. She continued her pursuit. We did not say one word. We just ran from one end of the village to the other a couple of times, repeating the swing-the-broom and the fake movements every time.

Some of the neighbors stepped out in front of their houses and watched us running from right to left and then again in the opposite direction. I was in the lead and Mom was chasing me with the broom in her hands, her pace slowing down. The neighbors watched us. They moved their heads from right to left, and then from left to right, like spectators of a very slow tennis match. The neighbors smiled and commented to each other, "Mother and daughter like to jog together." When Mom got tired of running, she stopped and walked to the house. I stayed outside a while longer until things calmed down and the broom was put away. The next day I went to school without the money.

Every day after school, when all classes were finished and the time had come for the students to go home, we took a break from the discipline that had held us tight during the school day. Our school was very close to the beach, within walking—or running—distance.

When school was over, the teachers walked all the kids to the front doors of the school and told us to go home. We were anxious to hear those last words. We had been dismissed for the day. We were free! We ran together toward the beach, screaming from the top of our lungs. We stopped running at the water's edge, took all our clothes off, and ran to the water. All those seven- and eight-year-old boys and girls were naked and screaming and splashing in the cold sea. I stayed where the waves broke, never wading into the water beyond my knees, but this was still the best way to end the school day.

This act of freedom did not last very long, though. The teachers ran after us as soon as they saw where we were going and what we were doing. They called to us from the beach, desperately trying to make their voices louder than ours: "That's enough! Get out of the water, get dressed, and go home!" We knew better than to stay in the water too long. As long as we got out of the water right when the teachers told us to, they let us get away with our daily innocent-yet-wild after-school skinny-dipping. We ran back to the beach, put our clothes back on, and went home, laughing and joking. I don't know if Mom ever knew about our little after-school adventure. I never told her about it; if I had, we would have been jogging around the village again.

My fear finally came true one day. I had not been able to bring any money to school to pay for my education, so I could not attend class anymore. It was a very sad day. I had learned the basics. I could read, write, and do basic math, but I was hungry for more.

I was not happy with this situation. All Koreans value education highly, and I was not getting enough of it. Of course, I did not want the neighbors to think that I was not educated, so I did not talk about what I was doing at school. I learned the best I could at home, reading on my own and learning from my sisters. I listened to adults when they talked about places they had visited and people they had met from other lands. I longed for a better education, but I would have to wait for better times. In the mean time, I occupied myself with other things, like building a wall.

The wind that blew toward the house from the beach was very cold sometimes. It hit our home head-on for long hours, stealing away any little warmth we had managed to create in the house with the small amounts of coal we had available. Sometimes the howling wind kept us awake at night.

Mom wanted to do something about the freezing wind. Just like the other neighbors had done, Mom wanted to build a stone wall around the house to shield it from the wind. This project would not be easy, but if Mom had decided to do it, I was certain that it would be done. We wouldn't be hiring anybody to build the wall; that much was obvious. The question was, who would help build the stone wall?

Mom told us about her project at dinner and that she wanted all of us to help. Dad was not home; it was up to us to help Mom. I jumped at the idea. I said I was ready to carry as many rocks as I could. If building a wall around the house would help keep it warmer, I was all for it. My brothers and sisters all said they would help, although they did not share my enthusiasm. Mom told us that we would begin building the wall the next day.

It was very hard work. It involved carrying an endless number of rocks from the beach or the mountain to our home, and then piling them up, forming a wall that would surround the house. We hauled small rocks, medium-sized rocks, and large rocks, all depending on our size and strength. Mom carried rocks, too and also directed where and how to place the rocks to make a solid wall. Nabi, my dog, ran back and forth around us as we carried the rocks. It was fun seeing him so energetic. I wished he could have carried some of the heavier rocks.

It took us a long time—I don't recall how long—but when we finished the wall, we were all very pleased with our hard work. We had worked diligently and our reward would be warmer nights. The wall, however, had a down side I had not noticed until it was finished.

"Don't cause any more trouble!"

My friend, who lived next door, and I liked to visit each other often. We just ran across the open space between our homes to quickly get together and play. But now the wall, which was taller than me, blocked the open path I used to cross to go to my friend's house. If I wanted to go play with her now, I would have to walk all the way around the wall to reach her home. What a waste of time!

I had to find a shortcut, I thought. I needed a quicker way to get over to my friend's. I looked at the wall, turning around to survey the whole construction. I was looking for a place that might provide me with some kind of shortcut. All sides of the wall looked very much the same. It was a straight wall, rising high above my head. I was sure that I could climb the wall to the top and then climb down to the other side without a problem, but Mom had forbidden me to climb it. She said that I might fall and get hurt. I also suspected that because she disapproved of my tomboy habits, she wanted to discourage me from doing any activity which, in her book, would be more proper for a boy.

I decided to obey Mom and crossed off wall-climbing as a shortcut.

But, there was something along the wall that looked like a promising shortcut. It was a well. We shared the well with my friend's family. The well was about half as tall as the wall, so it would be easy and safe to reach the edge. The well was not too wide, so I thought I could jump over it easily. I had found my shortcut. Next time I wanted to visit my friend I would jump over the well and be with my friend in a second. I didn't see a problem with that. Furthermore, Mom had not said anything about not jumping over wells; I had nothing to worry about. What could possibly go wrong?

One morning I was helping Mom pick potatoes from the small garden we had grown at one side of our home when my friend next door called me from the other side of the wall. "Come see this!" she said.

We were almost finished, so Mom said I could go. She expected me to walk all the way around the wall to meet my friend, but I was going to use my shortcut.

I swiftly climbed onto the edge of the well and jumped over its wide mouth. I missed the other end by a step. I tumbled all the way down the well.

"A-maaa!" I cried to my mom.

I had miscalculated the distance across the well; my legs were too short to jump over it safely. I splashed into the cold water at the bottom. I panicked—what if I drown?—but quickly reached the side and held on to the protruding stones on the inside wall of the well. The water was freezing and the stones were slippery, but I managed to hold on. Mom heard my cry and ran to the well. She looked into it and from below I could see her face, filled with panic. "Help me!" I cried.

Mom encouraged me to climb out of the well holding on to and stepping on the stones that covered the inner surface. I tried, but I failed. I was strong enough to climb a wall, but the wall was slippery and my hands were all muddy from pulling up potatoes. I climbed a few stones, but I slipped and fell back in the water. I grabbed onto the bumpy wall quickly. My body was shaking from the cold. I tried a few times, but there was no way to hold steadily. It was just too slippery. I kept falling back down.

Mom disappeared from my view at the top of the well for a few minutes and when she returned she had a rope in her hand. She dropped one end of the rope to me and told me to hold it tight. I held on to the rope as tight as I could as Mom pulled from the other end, trying to lift me out of my trap. It did not work. The rope slipped from my wet hands time after time as she tried to pull me out. I fell in the cold water again and again.

Mom disappeared from my view again. This time she came back with a friend. He was a young man and he had brought a ladder with him. He slid the long ladder inside the well and firmly tied his end of the ladder to something outside the edge of the well. The other end of the ladder reached the surface of the water where I was and the secured end above kept the ladder hanging in place. I could reach it easily and climbed up in no time.

By then, other neighbors had joined us around the well, curious about the commotion. When I appeared at the top of the well, Mom's eyes opened wide and she covered her mouth with her hands. I was a very impressive sight. My arms and legs were covered with bleeding scratches. I was bleeding from the front, the back, and the sides of my arms and legs. I looked at myself and I could not believe how much blood I had on me. Then I felt the pain.

Mom blurted out, "We don't have money! I cannot take you to the hospital!" She paused for a few seconds. "Did you learn your lesson?" she asked. "Now you know you cannot jump over the well."

The neighbors took care of me while Mom paced up and down, nervous and worried. She was too upset to care for my injuries. A couple of neighbors cleaned my wounds and applied home-made ointments and other remedies to help my scratches heal. The bleeding stopped soon. The scratches were mostly superficial, so the neighbors decided that I would probably heal myself, as long as I kept the wounds clean until they closed up.

Mom paced around me, shaking her head. "I don't know what to do with you!" she said. "Don't do anything like this again." Her command fell on deaf ears. I was destined to get into more trouble and cause Mom plenty of worry.

As I went to sleep that night, I thought about what Mom had said a while ago. If I followed my first impulse to do what came to my mind without thinking about the consequences, I might get in trouble or get hurt like I had been hurt in the well. My arms and legs hurt badly now; I could barely find a comfortable position on the blanket I was lying on. I finally lay still, resting on my back and looking at the thatched roof over my head. I closed my eyes and fell into deep sleep.

I recovered nicely from my well accident after a few weeks. My scratches healed and my bruises changed from deep purple, to yellow, to nothing, but I still have the scars on my legs to this day. I had also managed to stay out of trouble; I had not been involved in any more accidents or arguments with Mom since I had fallen into the well. Things had been running smoothly lately, which was fine with Mom. It was boring for me, though. There was nothing to do around the house besides chores with my sisters.

There was something puzzling about some of the chores, like folding clothes. My older sister Jung-Ja tried to show me how to fold our short-sleeve shirts, but soon she lost patience with me. When she said, "fold this half of the shirt to the right," I folded it to the left. When she said "fold it to the left," I folded it to the right. She thought I was joking first, but after I swore I wasn't joking and that I was trying to do it the way she showed me, she said, "You are dumb!" I laughed. I felt that way too.

The next morning I thought about the way I had responded to Jung-Ja's directions and it puzzled me even more. It was like I wanted to do one thing, but it came out just the opposite. It seemed so easy for my sister to do it, but I had to repeat the movement very consciously many times to get it right. I had to force myself to move in the opposite direction my body wanted to go. What was wrong with me?

I asked Mom. She did not tell me that I was dumb, like Jung-Ja had told me (What are sisters for, right?). Mom told me that it takes longer for some people to learn things, while others learn them in a shorter time. I just needed to practice until I did it right; that's all I had to do.

"Don't worry about that, just put more time into it," Mom said. "You are not dumb." It was a relief for me to hear Mom say I was not dumb, even though my sisters told me that all the time. When I had a harder time than other people learning to do something, I just put more time into it. Little did I know that this attitude would help me succeed later in life.

Summer was long and boring. To pass the time, I would lie down on the floor of my home and inspect the thatched roof, looking for something to catch my attention. I could see a whole zoo of bugs zipping around the branches and thatches that formed the roof. There were crawlers, hoppers, and slithering tiny creatures of many colors and shapes. If you were really quiet, you could even hear the scratchy noises they made as they moved among the thatches. The roof of my house was alive! Furthermore, I noticed one morning that it smelled really bad; that was something new.

I went outside the house and walked around it; I wanted to find out where the stench was coming from. The disgusting odor was unbearable when I was outside in the yard. I covered my nose and mouth with one hand and walked around the house, looking for the source of the sickening smell. I did not see anything unusual around the house, so I looked up at the roof. There, perching on the very top, were three or four big black birds. We call them "gamagi," which is the Korean word for crow or raven.

I wondered what had attracted them to my roof. I had to find out what they were doing and what the terrible stench was. I was alone; Mom and my brothers and sisters had not come back home yet. I did not want to wait until they returned home. Wouldn't it be a good surprise for all of them if I had solved the reeking mystery by the time they were back? I thought that was the best thing I could do. Besides, Mom never said that I couldn't climb on the roof.

I carried the ladder we kept at the back of the house all the way to the side wall and leaned it against the edge of the roof. I shook it a little to make sure it was stable, as I had seen my brother do a few times. When I felt confident that the ladder was stable, I climbed onto the roof. I was not scared at all, just very curious about what might be up there.

I walked on the roof slowly, checking that one step was firm before taking another. I walked toward the area where the big black birds perched together. When I got close, the gamagi turned their heads and looked at me, then hopped a couple of times, and flew away. They landed on top of the rock wall, watching me from a distance.

I took a few slow, measured steps and saw the cause of the stench. A rat had died on my roof. It seemed to have died a few days ago, because the birds had already been feeding on it and a few bugs crawled in and out of it. I got closer to the rat and with only two fingers I picked it up by its hairless tail. I walked back toward the ladder, quickly this time, eager to get down and show Mom that I had solved the mystery of the stinking roof top. But I did not reach the ladder. I fell through the roof all the way down to the kitchen floor.

Maybe I lost consciousness. I only remember sitting on the floor, still holding the rat by the tail and feeling very dizzy. I looked around to orient myself. Everything looked like it was covered in fog, and little stars danced before my eyes. My head hurt. I felt so dizzy and disoriented that I decided to lie down for a long while on the kitchen floor. I lost track of time.

When I woke up, I sat down again and waited to see if there were more sparkling stars around me or if I felt dizzy. I was feeling better and my sight was not foggy anymore. I had gotten back on my feet when Mom opened the front door and entered the kitchen. The first thing she saw was a sunbeam shining on the floor and me standing in the spotlight. She looked up and saw the hole I had left on the roof after falling through the thatch. "Why is there a hole in the roof?" she asked. "I wonder who did it." She looked back at me.

"I did it," I answered. I told her everything. I told her about the stench, the gamagi on the roof, and my decision to solve the problem, climbing onto the roof and finding out what had attracted the black birds. I showed her proof of my words—the half-eaten, reeking rat—and ended my story with the minor detail of me falling through the roof right onto the kitchen floor where I was standing. "No more stench, Mom!" I ended with a smile.

In spite of my good deed, Mom was very mad at me because I had climbed onto the roof all by myself. She could see that I was fine now, so she wanted to hit me with the broom for getting into trouble again. I was quick to leave the house and to stay out of her reach until she calmed down. The last words I heard from her as I ran toward the front yard were, "Don't cause any more trouble!"

I was never looking for trouble; things just happened.

Chapter 6

Rising Waters

Mom's urgent command woke me up in an instant. "We must leave the house now!"

I was getting on my hands and knees when Mom quickly lifted me up from the floor and held me tight in her arms. It was pitch black in the house and I heard a deep rumbling sound getting closer. My senses became sharper right away and I clearly felt something was very wrong.

Mom repeated her urgent command, "We have to get out, *now!*"

She ran to the front door and I held tight to her neck. My brothers and sisters stumbled behind us, unable to see where to go, trying to focus in the midst of the confusion and follow Mom. Mom opened the door and I thought we were doomed.

It was so dark outside that I could barely see, but I could hear very well. The rumbling sound got louder and a load of water rushed into the house. The water was moving so fast and was so strong that Mom and my brothers and sisters were pushed a few steps back and almost lost their balance. Mom called from the top of her lungs, "Let's go, quick!"

She lifted me above her head and struggled against the water, trying to leave the house. The water was rising fast. One moment it reached just below Mom's knees and the next the water was covering her waist. Mom and my siblings hustled, slipped, and hung on to each other and to whatever they could get their hands on to pull themselves out of the house. Once we were all out, a strong wind tried to push our bodies back into the house, tangled our hair, and forced us to close our eyes. But we were not going back in.

Mom led the way, running up the mountain, and all my siblings followed. We had to reach higher ground to be safe from the raging sea. Everybody in the village reached the top of the mountain. We had all gone through the same struggle, immersed in darkness and the deafening sound of the typhoon that had struck our island. For a while, we stayed put and listened carefully to the rumbling sound and to the splashing waves, trying to guess how high the water would get. Mom soon decided we needed to reach a safer place. She guided us to our uncle's home, which was on higher ground than ours and had not been flooded by the rising waters.

We spent the rest of the night at my uncle's, dry and warm, and as soon as the morning lights brightened the sky and we had confirmed that the storm had passed, we walked down the mountain to see what had happened to our home.

There was no home left to go back to. Everything was gone in the village. Where there once were houses and boats and fishing nets hanging from poles, now there was nothing but debris. Not one house had survived the violent surge. One of my brothers attempted to raise our spirits with a lame joke.

"Maybe our home has just been relocated," he said lightly. "Maybe it is somewhere down the path."

Nobody laughed. The house was gone and all our belongings with it. We had nothing left but what we were wearing.

My brothers and sisters and I looked at Mom. She seemed exhausted; her shoulders sagged and her eyes gleamed with suppressed tears. "What are we going to do, Mom?" we asked her. We knew that Dad had survived the surge, but we could only count on Mom.

"We need a new house," she answered matter-of-factly.

Slowly, our life resumed its usual routine. We lived with my uncle for some time until Mom found out that the Korean government was offering loans to people affected by the typhoon to buy new houses. Mom requested a loan and, like many other people in our village and others along the same coastline of the island, she used it to buy a new home a short distance from where our first house had been. We had a new, two-room home, but we also had burdensome loan payments that had to be paid promptly every month. Now, Mom had to struggle even more to finance the new home and to buy food. Nobody expected Dad to lend a hand. "How hard could things get?" I wondered. They got even worse.

After we moved to the new home, we saw Mom even less often. To make ends meet, Mom worked even harder and longer than before the typhoon and the new home. She now left home before dawn and returned late at night, but she always managed to bring something for us to eat. She spent incredibly long hours looking for jobs to provide us with meager basic needs. She dove as often as possible to harvest the sea. But things did not improve. The last blow to hit our family and the rest of Koje Do also came from nature. It happened slowly over two or three years, but at the end we were all irreversibly caught up in the disaster.

We noticed that our dinner plates had less food and fewer variations. We moved from having two or three vegetables to having just one. One night, we had only one vegetable. I am not sure what kind, but I remember there was just one small piece of it on each of our plates. That was going to be dinner that day. "There is no more," Mom replied when we asked her if there was something else to eat.

My siblings and I climbed the mountain every day looking for anything we could eat. We found plenty of "chick bu ri" or arrowroot and ate it frequently for a while. Soon, however, other villagers also climbed the mountain looking for the same plant and it became more and more difficult to find any kind of food.

Mom explained that the entire area was in a drought, and the drought was now in its third year. Farmers could barely grow any crops. Most of the crops died and there was less and less food every month. The drought was now so severe and had lasted for so long that a large area of the island was affected by famine. Things had never been so desperate in Koje Do before. If we had gone hungry one night a week before the drought, we now went to bed without dinner a few nights a week.

Mom could not even bring much food from the sea. Because the land was dry and did not provide any food, almost everybody on the island had turned to the sea for sustenance. There were so many people diving and fishing that fish, abalone, octopus, and seaweed became scarce after a few months. Not even the ocean was able to help us this time. At least I had Nabi to raise my spirits.

Nabi had been my companion for years, since Mom had brought him home as a little puppy. I cared for him, I fed him, I made sure he had enough water, and we played and exercised together. Nabi was my dog. He had yellowish-brown, short fur. He did not have any special markings; in fact he was a very plain-colored dog, but I really liked him.

Nabi grew into an energetic dog and I became very attached to him. He followed me into the mountains and even protected me from little creatures that, in his eyes, posed a threat to me, even though I didn't need his protection. He thought that his job was to care for me. Sometimes we would play on the beach, chasing the waves out to the ocean and then running back when the waves came in. We had a great time trying not to get wet. He accompanied me many times as I wandered on the beach, poking the wet sand looking for crabs and dreaming about a better future. Nabi shared my misfortunes and he uplifted my spirits. But one day, Nabi was not home anymore.

I came home and looked for Nabi as I usually did, but I could not find him anywhere. I called him, "Nabi, Naaaabi." I looked in the front and in the back of the house. I looked under the house, but he was not there. I stopped looking for him and asked Mom, "Where is Nabi?"

"He's not here," she said, looking away from me.

"Where is my dog?" I asked again, now getting suspicious that something bad might have happened to him and Mom did not want to tell me.

"I sold him," Mom said.

"What? Why?!"

"Mommy needed money to buy food, so I sold the dog," she said.

I could not believe she had sold my dog! I knew we were always short on money, so in a way—a very sad way—it was not really a surprise at all. Still, I was very sad. I cried even though I knew we had to have money for food no matter how much I loved my dog. I had lost Nabi. I would still have him if we had had more money.

That day we had soup and meat for dinner. "Soup *and* meat tonight?" I said.

"Yes," said my brother Chun Duk. "This is Nabi soup."

"What?" I said.

"Yes, this is dog soup," said Mom. She had sold Nabi to the butcher. He had killed Nabi and given Mom the meat.

"I don't want this soup!" I cried. "I am not going to eat my dog!"

I left the house and ran to the beach, crying the whole way. I was so angry I had lost my dog. I could not believe Mom had made soup out of *my* dog. I was so attached to him, and now I did not have him anymore. I did not want to have another dog or any other animal ever. I was not going to get attached to a pet and lose it just like that. It was too painful. That day I decided I was not going to get attached to any other pet. I decided I was not even going to touch an animal ever again.

Chapter 7

"We Live Together, or We Die Together."

One day when I was about nine years old, Mom did something she had never done before. She had climbed the mountain looking for edible plants to fix a meal, but the mountain had been practically cleaned out of any possible food. In desperation, Mom pulled a few pieces of bark from a tree and used them to make a "soup." She was inconsolable.

"This is not even food," she mumbled as she filled our bowls. "I cannot even feed my children. How can I end this misery?" she continued mumbling to herself. Mom was so upset that she never prepared "bark soup" again.

In her daily efforts to find at least one meal for her family, Mom traveled to other villages farther and farther away from home. It must have been during these travels that she heard about the possibility of finding better living opportunities in cities on the mainland, like Pusan. After hearing that jobs were better and that there was more variety to choose from, Mom pondered the possibility of moving inland, where she—and hopefully Dad—could increase their chances of making a decent living and bring better times to the whole family. But the decision to move was not hers. Dad was the head of the family, despite the fact that he did not assume the responsibility. He did not want to move and Mom was running out of options to feed her family.

One night, Mom returned home with only four or five potatoes for dinner. We had just a few small potatoes for a family of seven. That night, Mom did not eat so that the rest of us had at least something. She sat alone on a tree stump behind the house, looking at the ground with her fingers interlaced and resting on her lap. She was very quiet the entire evening and later that night I saw her kneeling on the floor, praying. Mom had never been that quiet before.

The next day, Mom called all of us. She placed one cup holding a clear liquid—it looked like water—in front of each one of us. She sat with us, placing a similar cup in front of herself. She then talked calmly, but did not look up. She told us that she had made a very difficult decision, but it seemed like it was the only thing she could do to end our misery once and for all. She felt that it was impossible for her to feed us anymore. She had tried very hard for a very long time and now felt she had exhausted all the options to find food. She had to admit—and this was very hard for her—that she could not take care of us anymore. She could not count on Dad to help. She was on her own, assuming all the responsibility, and she could not do it anymore.

She had considered many options; she had prayed every day and night. She was certain that she could never give us away for adoption or abandon us to manage on our own. She did not have the heart to break down the family—we would live together or we would die together. And living together we could not do anymore.

We were all going to drink the poison in the cup and die together with her. Death seemed the only way out. She did not want us to die, but what other option did she have? So, she told us to "lift your cups and drink this water tainted with rat poison."

We were all looking at Mom, our eyes wide open, our mouths dropped. I could not believe what she had said. I started to cry. "I don't want to die, Mommy! I want to live!" I cried.

"There is no other way," she repeated, her eyes wet with tears. "I have tried everything and for a very long time, but things have not gotten any better no matter how hard I tried. Things have turned for the worst. I have failed to feed my children. We will die together now and end our misery."

"I don't want to die!" I repeated. Mom stood up, holding her cup, and I kneeled at her feet, tugging at the bottom of her pants. "I want to live!" I looked at my brothers and sisters for support. "Help me! Do you all want to die?"

They all talked at the same time. It was hard to understand what each one of them was saying, but the words "I don't want to die" were repeated again and again. My older brother Hwa-Nam stood up, raised his hands, and the rest of us went silent.

"We will change things," he said, looking at Mom. "Starting today, Mom will not be alone looking for food for all of us. We will help her. We will all go to other villages and will look for any kind of job and earn money and buy food. We won't steal, but each of us has to come back home with something to eat. We will work together for our survival one day at a time."

Mom cried silently and sat down on the floor. It looked like a large, heavy load had been lifted from her shoulders. Now that she was sharing the load with her children, she could carry it much better. There was hope in the future if we all worked together.

We did not waste any time to implement our plan. We left home right away and each headed in a different direction; our minds were set on finding a means to get something to eat for dinner that night. We would survive one day at a time. That was the only thing that mattered now.

I walked around the village. I would have preferred to venture farther away, but because I was the youngest, Mom decided that it was best that I explore closer to home instead of far away. At the end of our street, I saw a group of people sitting and praying around a big, tall tree. I watched them from a distance and waited until they had finished their prayers and left before approaching the tree to get a closer look at what they had been doing.

At the base of the tree, somebody had left a bowl of rice. I was sure that it was an offering given with their prayers. Like all of us, the people that had gathered around the tree were affected by famine and prayed, asking for better weather that would end the drought. We all needed much better times.

I talked to the tree. "Tree, we have no food at all and I need this rice. I am going to take it, but I promise that I will bring something back in return when I can. We haven't eaten in days; we need this rice." I took the bowl home and gave it to Mom. She was very surprised.

"Where did you get this?" she asked. "Did you steal it?" she said frowning.

"I did not steal it. I took it from the tree down the street where a group of people had been praying. They left the rice before they left," I explained.

"I know that tree," Mom said. "We will bring food back to the tree when we can."

My brothers and sisters came back from their journeys. All of them had succeeded at finding something to eat. Some of them brought potatoes or roots. Mom lit a fire, put a pot on top to boil water, and cooked the vegetables and rice. She pureed them together and we had warm and thick soup that night. Nothing had tasted so good in a long time.

We decided to play a game and invited Dad to join us, but he preferred to go to his room to rest. Tears came to my eyes. I would have been completely happy if Dad had joined us and enjoyed the food, the game, the conversation, the laughs, but Dad went to his room and we continued our celebration, which is something we hadn't done in a very long time. We had hope; the future looked a little brighter that night.

Chapter 8

Dad

Our home had two bedrooms. All my brothers slept with Dad in one of the rooms and my sisters and I slept together with Mom in the other room. Sleeping arrangements were different in other homes. Usually parents slept together in one bedroom and the children occupied the other. We had had our own sleeping arrangements for a while now. Things were very tense between Mom and Dad; Mom did not want to sleep with Dad anymore.

We slept following our usual arrangements that night, women together in one room and men together in the other. In the morning, we woke up early to begin our customary search for jobs and food. We were all up except for Dad. We were waiting for him to eat breakfast with us before leaving. Mom had taught us that adults had to sit first and eat first and she made sure we didn't forget. It wasn't always easy for us to wait for the adults, but Mom would remind us by banging a spoon against the table if it looked like we were getting ahead of the adults.

Mom decided to wake him up. She walked to his room and found him lying down with his eyes closed. She knelt beside him and shook him by the shoulder, "Time to wake up!" she said.

Dad did not move. His eyes remained closed, his body still. Mom shook his shoulder again, a little harder this time. "Wake up!" she said louder. Dad did not move. Mom looked at his chest; it was not moving. She brought her ear to Dad's nose, but she did not hear a sound or feel his breath. Dad had died in his sleep.

Mom walked out of the room slowly and met all of us in the kitchen. "Dad is dead," she said. We all froze and stared at her. "I am so happy."

"You are happy Dad is dead?" one of my brothers asked.

"I am happy he died in his sleep. I am happy he did not suffer. His face looks peaceful and relaxed. He died without knowing it. I am also happy none of us suffered watching him die," Mom explained.

Dad had given us many hard times when he was alive, but his death was quick and painless. It seemed like by dying quickly and painlessly, he had tried to make up for all the tough times he gave us in life.

We never knew what killed Dad. We knew he had been careless with his health. He had drunk too much and he had smoked for years. He had also suffered the famine and the low times with us. He might have had a heart attack or a stroke when he was sleeping. We will never know.

I was shocked. "Dad is dead?" I thought. I was so sad. He was my Dad and I had wished many times our relationship would have been different, that he would have helped Mom so we could have been happier. I wished he had been more loving, that he had hugged me the day I was born. I respected Dad. I wished he could have joined us during our brief, happy family moments, such as when I found the giant octopus and we had food for a long time—even though it was the same food, three times a day—or during the rare occasions when we enjoyed a good story or a good laugh. Now he was gone and Mom had to make the decisions about our future as a family.

Dad's death made Mom look at our family future from a new perspective. Living in Koje Do had brought nothing but disaster to us. Job opportunities had declined drastically over the years during the annexation to Japan and continued declining later, during and after the Korean War, even for a person as resourceful as Mom. The typhoon had taken our home away and forced us to get a new house, committing to loan payments that were impossible to pay. The long drought had exhausted the land and indirectly exhausted the sea. People were starving. Dad had added a significant burden to our situation. He did not contribute in any way to ease Mom's load; on the contrary, his abusive behavior only made things worse. All these circumstances had created a situation that cornered Mom in a dead end; she was not able to feed her children, no matter how hard she tried. In Koje Do, she had almost died with all her children.

Now things looked different. Now, Dad was gone and Mom was in charge. She would make the decisions for the family now. We were in good hands. A few days after Dad's funeral, Mom gathered us together at home and told us of her plan for the future. Her attitude that day was positive and hopeful, even cheerful.

"We are going to leave Koje Do," she said matter-of-factly. "There is nothing here for us now; there is no future for you here. We are moving to Pusan, a big city on the mainland. In Pusan, we will have more opportunities to create a brighter future for all of us; there are more jobs there than there will ever be in Koje Do. We will leave in a few days."

I could not believe her words. We were leaving Koje Do, the only place I had ever lived? I had a million questions, but Mom was busy packing, so I left her alone for the moment. I wanted to ask: Where will we live? What does Pusan look like? Can I go to school there?

Mom's decision to move out of Koje Do and to Pusan would change my life in more ways that I could imagine at the time. The move turned out to be the first step in the journey that led me to who I am today, where I live, and the life I have. I am so happy and thankful to Mom for getting us out of Koje Do.

The first period of my life was about to end and I was nine years old. A new period was about to begin and it would be very different from anything I had experienced before. I was going to face a completely new world: the world of a growing city in a country heading toward modernization of its political, social, and cultural history. A new country that was ready to slowly accept changes in family traditions. Living in Pusan opened my eyes to better things the world had to offer, and the time became right for me to take on opportunities to achieve my childhood dream. We were going to Pusan!

PART TWO

LIFE IN THE BIG CITY

Chapter 9

Going to Pusan

Mom was definitely a good leader. She organized our move to Pusan quickly and efficiently. It made our move easier that we did not have too many things to pack and take with us. Mom got us ready in no time. She was well organized too; it was clear she had put a lot of thought into what we were going to do and how we were going to do it.

Jung-Ja did not move with us. She was married and stayed in Koje Do with her family. My brother Hwa-Nam joined the military, as was mandatory for all men about nineteen years old. My brother Choon-Duk, my sister Choon-Up, and I moved to Pusan with Mom. Mom and I moved to Pusan first, in the spring of 1965. We found a place for all of us to live and she found a job. Then, my brother and sister moved with us to the big city.

Pusan made a big impression on me. It looked nothing like my small village in Koje Do and nobody prepared me for it. Even if somebody had described the city to me before I saw it, I would have had a hard time imagining the tall buildings, the cars and buses, the new noises and smells, and the faster pace of a big city. None of those things existed in Koje Do. I faced a world in which people talked like me and looked like me, but they lived in places totally unfamiliar and worked and lived at a much different pace. In Pusan I saw my first bus, my first car and taxi, my first airplane, the tallest buildings, and my first lightbulb.

Choon-Ok in Pusan, between nine and eleven years old. The little girl smiles.

We spent the first night in Pusan at the house of one of my uncles. What a surprise when they turned on a small lightbulb hanging from the

Choon-Ok in Pusan, between nine and eleven years old.

ceiling! A bright light illuminated the whole room. I could see everybody and see where everything was. I realize now that it was not a very bright bulb, but compared to what we had in our home in Koje Do it was like night and day. In Koje Do we had no electricity. We used oil lamps to light up our nights. Pusan was a new world to me. If it weren't for the people, I would have thought I was not in Korea anymore.

My lifestyle changed and it was very hard for me to adapt. In Koje Do I was free to go wherever I wanted within the boundaries of the village and maybe a bit farther away sometimes. In Koje Do, I knew everybody in the village and we all watched out for each other. In Pusan, sometimes I felt like a prisoner in my home.

"The city is dangerous," Mom said. "There are bad people that take kids away and parents never see them again." The only way I could go anywhere was with Mom, my brother or sister, or with somebody else the family trusted. Otherwise, I had to stay home. I felt trapped.

It took time to adapt. Thankfully, my oldest sister Choon-Ja helped us find a home and familiarize ourselves with the new city. We met her friends and their families who also helped us. I was happy to meet new, friendly people, like Kim and his wife, who made us feel at home in their company. I babysat their baby daughter many times and even spent the night at their home watching the baby. We considered them good friends of our family.

On Christmas Eve, Kim knocked at our door. Mom opened the door and invited him in. He smelled a little bit of alcohol and was happy. It was almost Christmas, so Mom did not think his behavior was unusual. He was heading out the door when he asked if I would like to go to his home and play with the baby. I liked his little daughter and wanted to go. Mom said it was OK. She trusted him. Kim's home was about a twenty-minute walk from my house. He offered to carry me on his back,

Choon-Ok and Choon-Ja in Pusan.

piggy-back style. It sounded like fun and I knew it would be easy for him to carry me, because he was a large man and I was a skinny little girl. We laughed all the way to his house.

I realized that Kim was not going to his home. "Where are we going?" I asked. "This is not the way to your house."

"I need to stop at my sister's house to pick up something," he said.

"OK," I said innocently.

Kim's sister's house had two rooms—a kitchen by the entrance and a bedroom. He stepped into the kitchen and slowly put me down. Then everything turned into a nightmare.

"Get in the bedroom!" he ordered me.

I tensed up. He had never raised his voice at me. "What? Why?" I asked feeling scared.

"Get in there, I said!"

I ran to the room. He followed me and locked the door behind him. "Kim, why are you locking the door?" I did not understand what was going on, but felt more scared by the moment. Then he slapped my face with his enormous hand so hard my nose bled.

"Take your clothes off!" he yelled. I was confused and hurt. Why was Kim doing this?

"Take your clothes off!" he said and slapped me again.

I was terrified; my whole body was shaking. I took my shirt off and crossed my arms in front of my chest, ashamed.

"Take it all off!" he ordered.

"Not my pants," I said. He hit me in the head with his heavy hands and I felt dizzy.

"Take it all off or I will hit you again!"

I took all my clothes off and crossed my legs, ashamed of being completely naked. I knew now that something was completely wrong. I did not understand yet what he wanted, but I knew this was bad.

"Why are you doing this, Kim?" I screamed and cried. I yelled, "Let me go! What are you doing?"

He shoved me against the wall and I hit my head, screaming in pain and panic. "Lie down on the floor and shut up or I will hit you again!"

I could not stop screaming. I was terrified of him, of his violence, and of what might happen next.

"Shut up or I will kill you!" he said. He grabbed my neck with his hand and tightened his grip. I remember struggling for air. I stopped screaming and slowly lay down on my side on the hard floor with my legs crossed and pulled against me, and my arms folded over my chest.

"Open your legs," he ordered standing over me.

He unbuttoned his pants. My body was shaking uncontrollably. Why was he doing this? I screamed again, begging him to let me go. He slapped my face twice so hard I thought I would pass out.

"I will kill you if you don't shut up! Open your legs."

I closed my eyes, sobbing, and obeyed, shaking all over. When I felt him trying to get inside me, I panicked again and screamed. It hurt so much! He stood up and walked toward the kitchen, returning with a large knife in his hand. He touched my throat with the tip of the knife.

"I will use it if you don't stay quiet."

I did not say another word. I thought I was going to die. He leaned over me and hurt me again.

A woman screamed over Kim, "What are you doing?! Are you out of your mind?" It was Kim's sister.

I opened my eyes and looked at her. "Help me," I whispered. Then I screamed, "Help me!"

She pulled him up and furiously hit his face with her fists, cornering him against the wall. She yelled at him and hit him with her hands and feet. I was free! I jumped on my feet and ran out the door into the freezing night, naked. I did not stop running until I reached my home. I did not even feel the bitter air brushing my bleeding body or the hard, frozen ground on my bare feet. I just wanted to go home to my Mom. I pounded on the door with both my fists until Mom opened the door. "Kim did it," I said and passed out.

I woke up in the hospital. I was bleeding all over my body and had bruises and cuts. I spent two days in the hospital. I did not want to see anybody but my family. For a long time, I was scared of tall men.

Mom told me that when my oldest brother and sister realized what had happened to me, Hwa-Nam ran to Kim's sister's house and my sister Choon-Ja rushed to the police station. Hwa-Nam found Kim still in the house, beating his sister. Hwa-Nam told Mom later that he could not believe his eyes when he entered the room. There was blood everywhere on the walls and on the floor from Kim's sister's wounds. Hwa-Nam was furious! He fought Kim until the police arrived and separated them. Kim went to jail and stood trial a few months later. To my despair, the judge wanted my testimony for the trial.

The last thing I wanted was to relive that night, describing it to others. "I don't want to tell anybody what happened, Mommy!" I was afraid to see Kim again in the trial. I was ashamed of telling anybody what happened.

"I won't tell you to go or not to go to the trial to give your testimony," Mom said. "It is your decision. I think you should go so he gets the maximum sentence, but you have to decide if you will go or not."

I thought about it for many days. My body had healed but my memories of the terror, the pain, and the feeling of helplessness and certain death still haunted me. I did not want to see Kim ever again. But if I did not go, he would receive less time in jail and maybe hurt another little girl like me when he got out. On the other hand, if I told the judge what happened, Kim would get a full sentence. I am not sure how long a full sentence was, maybe ten years. Mom said that my whole family would be in the trial with me. Mom and my sisters and brothers would support me all the way. I decided to testify.

I don't remember the trial well. I can only recall that I did not look at Kim's face at all and that my sister Choon-Ja was infuriated and jumped on his face, scratching him with her nails. Kim went to jail with the maximum sentence.

This was one of the most terrifying experiences of my life and probably one of the reasons I am the person I am today. The way I react to abuse, bullying, and unfairness probably relates to my own experience. This experience is probably one of the reasons my brother Hwa-Nam was so protective of me. He must have felt terrible for not being able to protect me from such a monster.

Before I worked on this memoir, only my family, including my husband and daughters, knew about it. I don't like to talk about it at all because when I do, I relive in my mind the horrible scenes, the pain, and the terror I felt. I almost did not include it in my memoir, but my daughters convinced me to do it. They think if other young girls and women read about this experience, they will be more aware of this type of situation. The worst part is that I trusted Kim. I always mistrusted strangers, but my whole family knew Kim and his wife and I was his daughter's babysitter. He used this trust to take advantage of me. It took me a very long time to learn to trust again. I think one of the best things girls and women can do is to support each other, and go out in groups, not alone.

Time passed and our life in Pusan continued.

Chapter 10

Life Goes On

In Koje Do we had our own house all to ourselves, but in Pusan we lived in one rented room. That was another big change, because now our living area was smaller and when it rained hard, water leaked through the roof and we had to place one pot here and another one there to keep the water from flooding the room. Mom would try to make our lives happier, singing a song to the beat of the raindrops filling the pots. In spite of our efforts, sometimes I woke up in the morning with my clothes soaked with rain water that had overflowed the pots or just fallen on the floor. We asked the landlord to fix the roof many times, but he didn't.

Sometimes, Mom told us a scary story to help us forget tough times. She was a great storyteller and knew many stories. One night Mom told us a story about a tiger, a thief, a persimmon, and a farmer's crying baby boy.

The first photo of Choon-Ok and her mother, Pusan, 1968.

The farmer had a three-year-old boy that cried very late every night. He cried so loudly that it could be heard far out into the forest. His mom tried to quiet him by giving him fruit and candy, but nothing worked. He just cried louder each time his mom tried to quiet him.

One day, his mom decided to try another tactic. She tried to appeal to the baby's fear of tigers instead of his love for candy.

"Don't cry little baby, because a hungry tiger might hear you and want

81

to eat you," she said. But the baby boy did not seem to care about the tiger. He cried even louder at his mother's warnings.

That night, a hungry tiger descended from the mountain, looking for food. The tiger loved to eat cows and he came to the farmer's barn, looking for a tasty cow. He heard the baby crying and walked to the front door of the house to investigate what it was. He heard the baby's mother talking to the baby. "Don't cry little baby because a hungry tiger might hear you and want to eat you," she said.

The tiger thought proudly, "I'm the most powerful animal in all the mountains. All creatures shiver with fear when I roar and hide when I come down from the mountain."

As the tiger listened, he noticed that the baby cried louder when his mom told him to fear the tiger. But when the mother said, "Stop crying and I will give you a persimmon," the baby stopped crying immediately.

The tiger was surprised and then thought, "What is a persimmon? Is something more powerful than me? It can make this baby stop crying when mentioning my name cannot!"

The tiger got scared and ran to hide in the barn to make sure the persimmon didn't get him. At the same time, a thief had come into the barn to steal the farmer's cow. It was so dark that night that neither the thief nor the tiger could see very well. The thief was using his hands to help him find the cow when he touched the back of the softest cow he had ever felt.

"This must be the best cow in the entire province," he said. He climbed onto the tiger's back, thinking it was a cow, and faced the tiger's tail.

The tiger felt the weight on its back and thought, "Oh no! It's a persimmon!" He took off running and yelled, "Don't kill me Persimmon, please, don't kill me!" As the tiger ran out of the barn, the sun was coming up and the thief saw that he had jumped on the back of a huge, ferocious tiger.

"Don't eat me Mr. Tiger!" he said, grabbing the tiger's tail harder.

"Please don't kill me, Persimmon!" said the tiger, running faster toward the mountain. The harder the thief grabbed the tiger's tail, the faster the tiger ran. They ran off into the mountains, yelling at each other, "Please, don't eat me Mr. Tiger!" "Please, don't kill me, Persimmon!"

We had a good laugh at the thief and the tiger story. Mom was a wonderful storyteller. We drifted off to sleep after one of the best evenings at home in a long time. Life was not easy in the big city, but on clear nights we could see stars through the roof. We lived in that room for about a year before moving to another room. We moved many times from one room to another while living in Pusan.

Pusan was not our permanent home. Even though the city offered more job opportunities than Koje Do, it was not easy for Mom to find a job, and many she did find were temporary. We moved from one place to another, following Mom's jobs. As before, Mom and I moved first and then my brother and sister would follow. Being constantly on the move kept me out of regular school. I was disappointed, but there was nothing I could do. I had to follow Mom as she searched for better jobs from one place to another. She knew that education was important, but it was more important that we have a regular income. Schooling had to wait. My first three years in Pusan and nearby cities went by fast with all the moving from one place to another. It was hard to settle down and to make friends.

Mom focused on retail sales when we were in Pusan. From clothing to soy sauce, she sold it in markets to earn a living. I helped her. Mom would go to the soy sauce factory, buy large jars, and bring them home. We would fill small bottles with soy sauce and sell them in the market. Mom also went to the mountain around Pusan and collected "dorichi root," which is similar to ginseng. We packed it in small portions and sold it in the market, too.

I think that Mom might have inspired my brother Choon-Duk and me to explore some retail business on our own. It was a very hot summer and my brother and I wanted to make money to help Mom. We found a small wooden box and filled it with ice and sweet

bean-flavored popsicles we bought at the store. My brother carried the box in his arms and I waved a popsicle in each hand as we walked the streets, advertising the cool treats. "Popsicles, popsicles!" It was so hot that we thought the frozen, sweet popsicles would be easy to sell. We were not lucky that day.

Choon-Ok in the hills near her home in Pusan.

We had just sold two popsicles when the sun hid behind large, dark clouds and thick rain poured over the city. People ran for cover; nobody wanted popsicles anymore. Choon-Duk and I took cover under a roof and waited for the rain to stop, but the rain persisted. It was still very hot, and to our dismay the popsicles began to melt. My brother and I looked at each other. What could we do?

We sat on the floor and Choon-Duk gave me one popsicle and he had another one. We didn't want the popsicles to go to waste. I loved popsicles because they tasted so sweet and fruity. We usually did not eat them because they were expensive for us, but now they were melting. We ate a second one, then a third one, savoring every lick and every bite of the sweet treat. The rain continued to pour and the heat did not ease up. We ate them faster and faster before they melted. Soon, we had finished the box of popsicles.

I must have eaten more than ten of them. We waited under the roof for the rain to stop and that's when I started to feel sick. My stomach hurt badly. My brother had to carry me in his arms all the way back home and I cried the whole time. I did not want to go home and tell Mom what had happened. I had eaten too many popsicles; I had gotten sick, and we had not sold enough to help Mom. In spite of our bad luck that day, I got lucky, because Mom was not home when we arrived. I decided not to tell her about our failed popsicle sale or my stomach ache. It was a secret between Choon-Duk and me.

Not long after our failed popsicle sale, a tragedy clouded our days. Bad news arrived from Koje Do that my sister Jung-Ja, who was a haenyo like Mom, had died in a diving accident. The other fishermen and haenyo said a shark had attacked and killed my sister while she was diving, but Mom never believed them. In all the years she had been diving, she had never seen a shark. That had never been a concern of haenyo divers in the area for as long as she could remember.

She believed instead that my sister had died when explosive charges had gone off underwater. Fishermen sometimes used explosives to capture large numbers of fish at a time. This was an illegal practice, but still it continued. Mom thought my sister might have triggered an explosion accidentally while diving. Maybe Jung-Ja had tried to grab abalone or seaweed, but found an explosive instead, setting it off accidentally. Mom was devastated. She promised she would never dive again. She felt that the sea had taken her daughter away in exchange for all the food Mom had taken from the sea throughout her years of diving.

Mom went to Koje Do for a few days. She dove, looking for her daughter's body, but only found one finger. My sister had left two boys. One was five years old and the other three months old. Because of her grandsons, Mom decided not to go to court to contest my sister's cause of death. If Mom went to court, her son-in-law could go to jail, because he was involved in illegal fishing using explosives. If he went to jail, the children would be left without a parent to care for them. So Mom gave it up. She did not bring the issue to court for the sake of her little grandchildren. She decided it was better for them to be with their father. She returned to Pusan and we moved on, but Jung-Ja's loss was hard for Mom.

After Mom returned to Pusan, it seemed that for a while she might lose her mind. She would call Jung-Ja's name in her sleep or get up and run out of the house looking for her. I tried to stop her, but she was too strong. I would pull her arm to make her stay, but she would easily escape from my grip. Occasionally we would run after her as she left the house, but Mom would disappear and we couldn't find her. This worried us very much because there was a curfew in Pusan at the time. During that time, because of the tense relations with North Korea, the government had declared that no civilians could be on the streets between midnight and 4 a.m. If you were out, you might be considered a spy and shot on the spot. We feared for Mom's life every time she ran away from home during the curfew. Fortunately, she always came back home the next day without being harmed. About a year after Jung-Ja's death, Mom settled down and returned to her normal emotional state of mind—in control, energetic, and no-nonsense. She mourned my sister for a long time.

Chapter 11

When I Discovered Martial Arts

When I was twelve years old, I discovered martial arts, and nothing has changed my life as profoundly as this. My first encounter was with Tae Kwon Do. There was a school near my home and I watched students practice every day as I walked by the school. The more I watched them, the more interested I became, but I knew I could not join the school because we did not have the money. But I did not have to pay to watch or to wish I could be one of the students in white uniforms kicking and punching. That was the only martial art I knew at the time; I had not heard of Kuk Sool Won yet.

My sister brought Kuk Sool Won into my life at about this time. Choon-Up and Kuk Sool Won Chief Master In Sun Seo wanted to get married. My sister brought Chief Master to our home, introduced him to Mom, and they expressed their wishes to get married. Mom approved of him and gave her permission for their engagement.

One day Choon-Up took me to see Chief Master's school and for the first time I saw the practice of Kuk Sool Won. If Tae Kwon Do had caused an impression on me, it was nothing compared to what I saw in Chief Master's school. The Tae Kwon Do school near my house only had about ten people practicing at one time, but the Kuk Sool Won school had forty to fifty students, maybe more. Everybody was wearing a black uniform. When I saw people practicing Tae Kwon Do, they were kicking and punching. It surprised me that Kuk Sool students were doing many more things. I was shocked. They were not just kicking and punching; they were throwing each other and doing joint locks, using traditional weapons, and creating beautiful forms. I just sat and watched them for hours. I was fascinated! This appealed to me immensely.

I tried to share my enthusiasm with Choon-Up, but she was not interested in practicing Kuk Sool. There were women practicing in the school with men side-by-side. Some women were high school students while others were about twenty years old. All together, there were about ten women practicing among about fifty men. Some were really good at it. My heart beat faster. It was exciting to see women practicing with traditional Korean weapons. I thought, if I just could join them. . . .

When my sister came home I approached her with determination. "I want to go there and practice!" I told her.

She was quite surprised by my request and looked at me frowning. "No, you are not going in there," she said. "I would be embarrassed if you, my sister, practiced there."

"Why not?" I replied. "I want to go. I want to practice like the other women in the school."

Choon-Up thought for a minute. "You are too young; you cannot go in there."

Mom had heard us arguing and came to the room. As soon as she knew the reason for our discussion, she raised her voice. "No good women go in there and do that kind of stuff; only men do that. Martial arts are not for women," she said. As always, Mom's comment settled the discussion—for the moment at least. I decided to wait for a better time to bring it up again.

The issue came up again when my brother Choon-Duk joined Kuk Sool. I could not believe it! I was so upset I cried. "How come he can practice and I cannot?" I complained between sobs. "It's not fair!"

Mom got up, hands on her hips, eyebrows touching. "Go up the mountain and get some water!" Mom always asked me to do that, because we did not have running water in our home. But this time, I knew she just wanted to get my attention away from practicing Kuk Sool. I brought a couple of pails of water to the house and sat them in the kitchen. Then I asked Mom again to let me practice Kuk Sool. I argued that my brother would be there to watch me. There were other women too, so I wouldn't be the only woman among many men. I really liked Kuk Sool and I wanted to practice it now. She did not change her mind. She just said, "No, no, and no," and she gave me more chores to do.

I persisted, trying to convince Mom to let me practice. I wanted to do what my brother Choon-Duk was doing. Ever since I was a little girl in Koje Do, whatever Choon-Duk did, I wanted to do, too. Now my brother was practicing Kuk Sool, but I could not do it with him. I could only follow him to class every day and watch him and the other students. That was as close as I could get to Kuk Sool training for the time being. I had to wait two years before I could join him on the practice floor.

After my sister Choon-Up married Chief Master, I again brought up the issue of joining Kuk Sool. We were family now with a Kuk Sool master, and this might change Mom's mind.

"I want to practice Kuk Sool. I want to learn something," I insisted. I am sure Mom was very tired of listening to my constant begging.

She sighed and said, "Ask Chief Master, your 'Hyung Bu,'" which means brother-in-law in Korean.

I did not think twice about asking Chief Master. I had no problem doing it. I went to his home and, as soon as I saw him, I said very seriously, "I want to start practicing Kuk Sool."

He looked at me and asked, "Are you sure? Are you absolutely sure? This is a very important request because if you start, you cannot stop. You cannot drop out of class. This would be a life-long commitment. Are you ready to dedicate your life to Kuk Sool Won? "

"Why not?" I asked.

"Why don't you think about it more? This decision should not be made lightly," Chief Master said.

"I want to practice Kuk Sool with the other students in your school. I have wanted to do it since Choon-Duk started two years ago. I am sure this is what I want," I replied.

"Kuk Sool practice requires dedication on your part. You really need to set your mind to it, because once you start Kuk Sool Won, you have to continue," he said, looking me in the eye.

"I won't stop!" I promised. "I'll continue all my life." At the time, I just wanted to start; I didn't care what happened later. I was hungry for it. It was more than wanting to do what my brother was doing. I had never wanted to do something as much as I wanted to practice Kuk Sool. I had to commit for the rest of my life? So be it. I wanted to begin right away.

Chief Master asked me again, "Do you promise me that you would never stop practicing once you start? Are you ready for this type of commitment?"

My Mom, Choon-Duk, and my sister Choon-Up were there with us; I could only think that I was very close to fulfilling my two-year-long dream. "I won't stop," I said. "I'll continue, I'll continue!"

Choon-Ok with Chief Master and Choon-Up, shortly after Choon-Ok started practicing Kuk Sool Won.

"OK," said Chief Master. "Come tomorrow."

I could not believe it! I had permission to start Kuk Sool practice. I went to the school the next day. I was excited and full of expectation. I was going to be on the practice floor learning all the kicks, punches, techniques, and forms I had seen the other students practice for so long. One day I would learn to master the sword and the knives, my favorite weapons. I was going to be one of them now.

When I arrived in the school, the "do jang," Chief Master gave me a black uniform and a white belt. I joined practice right away and I was really into it. It was very interesting; I liked it. In one week I learned a few beginner's techniques, called Ki Bon Soo, and a beginner's form, called Ki Cho Hyung. I was very happy.

I was also a bit concerned that it was taking me longer than my classmates to learn the techniques and forms right. The other students only needed to see the instructor demonstrate a technique once, maybe twice; but not me. I saw it once, but did not get it immediately. I had to see it many more times than the other students and practice much longer to get the movements right. My problem was puzzling to me. If they stepped to the right, I stepped to the left. If they grabbed with the left hand, I grabbed with the right. It was the same thing that had happened to me when I was a little girl helping my sister fold clothes. I did not understand why this was happening to me and not to the other students.

Some of the students laughed at me because of my mistakes. I laughed along with them; I did not want them to see I was actually puzzled and upset about this. I was so angry at myself that I practiced harder and harder. I was determined to get it. I remembered what

Mom had told me years ago when I told her about my difficulties learning to fold clothes properly, "You just need to practice longer; that's all." I was going to learn it. I was going to practice ten, no, a hundred times more than anybody else until I got it. It was my secret. I did not tell anybody about this difficulty for years.

Chief Master organized frequent public demonstrations of our practice to attract new students to the do jang. Students of all levels participated in the demonstrations at public schools. I had been in Kuk Sool for about a week when Chief Master planned a demonstration. He had scheduled an advanced female student to participate, but she could not attend for some personal reasons I do not remember. Chief Master wanted to have at least one woman in the demonstration because women's participation usually attracted a large crowd. He stood on the practice floor, arms crossed on his wide chest, looking at all the students practicing.

I was practicing the first techniques I had just learned by myself. I was repeating over and over, Ki Bon Soo number one, number two, and number three. It was not easy. I confused my steps sometimes. I had to step forward with my right foot, but I stepped forward with my left. I backed up and tried again, and again. I remember what Mom had told me: "It takes longer for some people to learn things others learn quickly. Don't worry about it. Keep trying until you get it right." I needed many repetitions if I wanted my forms and techniques to look as good as the advanced students' techniques.

Chief Master locked his eyes on me. "Come here," he called me. "Do Ki Bon Soo one, two, and three." He asked my brother to assist me by being my partner and falling or "nak bub" when I performed the technique on him. My brother Choon-Duk and I demonstrated for Chief Master. He taught me a couple of new techniques. Now I knew five techniques. Chief Master watched my brother and me repeat Ki Bon Soo one through five a few times. "OK. You go to the demo today," he told me matter-of-factly.

"What?" I said. "I do not know how to demo!"

"Well, I just showed you the techniques. Do them in the demo," he said calmly.

That was the end of it. I was going to demo. There was no arguing with Chief Master; if he said you were going to demo, you went and did the techniques he told you to do.

I went to the demo and my entire body was shaking. There were so many people watching! "I cannot do this," I whispered to Chief Master.

Choon-Ok during a public demonstration.

He looked me in the eye. "I said you do it! You cannot refuse to do what I told you to do!" he said, and left me on the demonstration floor with my brother.

The demo began and all the students performed their assigned techniques and forms, but I was frozen. The crowd applauded and cheered. My brother said, "Go!" and I stopped thinking about how worried I was and instead thought about my techniques. I focused and performed Ki Bon Soo one, two, three, four, and five. Then, we did them again. My brother did good nak bub every time, falling hard against the floor and yelling to release his energy ("ki op"). I performed ki op too and it helped to release my tension. In no time it was all over.

Chief Master came to the demo floor and congratulated us. He said to me, "You did a good job. Now every time we have a demo, I want you to be part of it."

I was happy that everything had turned all right, but another demo? I had mixed feelings about it. Soon, however, I lost my fear of public demonstrations. Chief Master wanted to visit and perform demos at about three hundred schools. And he wanted to do this in one year. There were only two women at the time doing demos for the school, and I was one of them. I had intensive demo practice that soon erased my fear of public presentations.

School demos began one summer and ended the next summer. In that year, we did our demos in blazing sun, drenching rain, or freezing temperatures. The weather was not important because we could not skip days; we had to demo a few schools every day to reach our goal of three hundred demos. On a few occasions we started the demo under sunny skies, and finished in pouring rain. The students watching us would run for cover inside the school building. We saw them bunched up around the windows to see us, because we did not stop the demo. We continued despite our soaked uniforms, the blinding rain, and the slippery ground. It was funny sometimes because our thin uniforms were so soaked in rain they stuck to our skin, so when one student threw another it looked like he was flinging a wet cloth around, tracing a stream of water in the air. These were some of the best times I remember from my training. They were very tough times, but they were exciting and fun and I ended up looking forward to doing several demos every day.

A few days after my first demo with my brother, Chief Master approached me during practice to comment on my techniques. "Do them harder," he said. I put more energy into it and threw my brother harder. And he was mad at me! My brother glared at me, his eyes like flames. Thinking back, I believe that my brother would not have been so upset if I had been a beautiful girl and not his sister. It was a typical older brother-younger sister problem.

"But Chief Master told me to do it reazlly hard," I told my brother.

"We'll see later," he said. He turned his back and went to the other side of the do jang to practice.

Every time I performed my techniques harder on Choon-Duk, he got upset with me during demonstrations. I decided to tell Chief Master about it.

"I cannot demo on my brother," I told him. "Every time I do it he wants to kill me!"

Chief Master observed us practicing together and in the next demo I had a new partner. I did not demo on my brother anymore. This is how I started Kuk Sool Won. I was fourteen years old.

Chapter 12

Real-Life Self-Defense

Mom had much to say against me practicing Kuk Sool at the beginning, but after my sister married Chief Master and my brother began his practice, she did not say anything else for some time. I had given my word to Chief Master that I would not quit practicing once I started, so Mom realized that I was committed. I went every day to practice, morning and afternoon, and felt happy that I was learning something I had a passion for. I guess Mom saw all this and decided that it had been a good decision for me to join Kuk Sool. She probably thought that it kept me busy and out of trouble.

However, a couple of years after I had started practicing, she again brought up her concern about me doing an activity that, in her mind, was better suited for men. I had been practicing hand training, which consists of hitting hard surfaces like stones with the palm of your hands. I would sit down in the do jang for hours and hit the stone until my hands were red and throbbing. Sometimes, the skin on my palms would crack and bleed, making the stone bloody. I did not stop the palm training; I wrapped a bandage around my palm and continued hitting the stone. I had my own individual stone that I practiced on for years. It was stained with dry blood that had leaked through the bandage. Years later, after I was married, I looked for my stone during one of my trips to Korea, but could not find it.

One consequence of this training was that my hands looked bigger and rougher. Mom did not like this change. She took my hands in hers and said, "Look at your hands! How do you expect to find a husband with these hands? When you marry, your husband won't like your hands. They look like a man's hands. They are not soft and smooth like women's hands should be. You better stop training or you will never find a husband."

Maybe Mom's concern was that she did not see the point of doing

hand training. Maybe I should have explained to her that hand training helped me become a better martial artist, making my hands stronger and tougher. I was going to be able to strike with more power and
I would be less likely to hurt my hands when I hit something hard.
Maybe if I had explained this to Mom, she would have understood why
I wanted to do hand training and stopped arguing with me. Or, maybe
she would not have cared about me getting stronger, tougher hands.

Either way, I did not care if my hands looked like a man's hands. I
was not going to stop the training I had waited so long to start. If this
was what I had to do in Kuk Sool, I was going to do it. I continued my
hand training despite Mom's complaints. I think Mom had not fully
realized how important and useful Kuk Sool was to me. It was good,
not just for me, but for others around me, including her.

Mom had a definite change of heart about me practicing Kuk Sool
after an incident in the market. One sunny morning, she was sitting on
the sidewalk at the market by herself, selling soy sauce and clothing to
passersby. I was not with her at the moment because I was picking up our
lunch. A couple of young men approached Mom and demanded money
from her. They were local gang members who were trying to extort money from her and other merchants. "You need to pay us to sit down here.
You need to pay us for the right to use this place!" they demanded.

Mom did not comply. She stood up straight and argued with them;
she had a fast temper, too. Things heated up as the men insisted on
receiving payment and raised their voices, threatening her. Other
merchants began to gather around Mom and the men; yelling and
tension filled the market. But Mom was not intimidated by a couple
of young men. I was coming back with our lunch, and from a distance
I saw Mom holding one of the men by the collar of his shirt, shaking
him, while the man was also holding her by her clothes and pulling
her close to him. He had had enough of my mom's arguing and was
raising his hand to punch her.

I reacted automatically. I dropped our lunch, rushed through the
crowd, and just before he threw his punch, I pushed him hard on his
chest with my hands, separating him from Mom.

"Leave her alone!" I ordered him, standing my ground.

The man regained his balance, looked at me, smirking, and slowly
stepped in my direction, clenching his fists. I wonder now what he
was thinking at that moment. He definitely underestimated me.
Korean women should be submissive, he might have thought. Perhaps

he wanted to teach me to be submissive. I was ready for him. I was not going to back up. He had threatened Mom.

He walked slowly toward me, ready to punch. I grabbed one of his hands and did Ki Bon Soo number two, a technique I knew very well after a couple of years of training. It was one of the techniques I had demonstrated in my first demo with my brother. But this was no demo. This was the real thing. I did not think; I just did Ki Bon Soo number two. I took his hand, bent his elbow, swung under his arm, bent it on his back and kicked one of his legs down. He fell on his knees, screaming. I held him down a few seconds, applying pressure on his arm, pushing him down with my body while he continued screaming. I let him go quickly and stood back, fixing my eyes on him, ready to defend myself again if he wanted to retaliate.

He could not believe what had happened to him. He had never suspected that a young woman, only 5' 4" tall and thin as a stick could control him and make him feel so much pain. He looked confused, and when he stood up and the people around him pushed him away, he left without complaining. I relaxed and looked at Mom to see if she was OK.

Mom was even more surprised than the young man that had attacked her. She looked at me and said, smiling, "It worked! What you have learned has worked!"

But she changed her tone right away. "Now, try not to use it often and stay out of trouble," she said with a frown. That was my mom.

Choon-Ok enjoying nature.

"Mom, if someone wants to hurt you I cannot just stand and watch them do it. I need to do something to help you out of trouble," I replied.

After this incident, she was very proud of me. She told everybody what I had done to protect her and that I was going to Kuk Sool Won school. All the people in the market looked at me and congratulated me: "You did a good job!"

After the incident in the market, Mom did not complain about me practicing Kuk Sool anymore and I settled into a nice routine. I woke up around 5:00 a.m. and, while Mom cooked breakfast, I jogged up the mountain right behind our home, all the way to the top. Many people exercised at this early hour, even though it was dark. I jogged through the mountain trails and drank fresh water from springs. I also practiced kicking and punching and forms on my own and then ran back home at sunrise, around 6:00 a.m.

This was the perfect time for me to repeat, repeat, and repeat techniques and forms I had difficulty with. I focused on doing the correct movements. I had to focus completely on what I was doing. Left, not right. Wrong. Do it again.

Sometimes frustration got to me. I just sat on the ground and hit it with my fists. Why was it harder for me? I was angry with myself, but I would not give it up. If I did, my life would be empty and my future bleak. Did I want that kind of future? I realized I had no other option. I shoved those defeatist thoughts aside and continued practicing.

When I returned home, Mom had breakfast ready for the whole family. We ate together and then left the house to our daily jobs. My job was to go to Kuk Sool school. I followed this routine all year long, even in winter when mornings were bitter cold and pitch black.

I was never tired; I had plenty of energy and was doing something all the time. I spent most of the day practicing Kuk Sool, but I also

Choon-Ok helped her mom with chores. Notice the kimchi jars in the back.

helped Mom sell her merchandise in the market, shopped for groceries, or helped with chores around the house. There was no idle time at all, especially when I was at Kuk Sool school. The first class of each day was at 5:00 a.m. for people who had to go to work and wanted to practice before heading to their jobs. I practiced in the 7:00 a.m. to 9:00 a.m. class. This class was large and in winter the do jang felt very cold. We did not have a heating system like we have in our school today, not even a small furnace to warm ourselves. After an hour of practice, my feet were so cold they hurt badly. They hurt so much that I would sit down on the straw mat covered with a plastic tarp that was our practice floor and rub and hit the bottom of my feet, trying to bring some feeling and warmth back to them.

In the summer, we struggled with the heat. There was no air conditioning or even a fan in the do jang in those days. Whatever the temperature was outside, that's what it was inside, and sometimes it was even hotter with all the students practicing. We trained with temperatures in the 80s or 90s inside, without even a light breeze blowing through the window. The do jang also would smell bad with so many people practicing and sweating. But we did not complain. If you did, you had to leave. I focused on my training and soon I forgot the heat or the cold and the pain or the bad smells in the intensity of practice.

Choon-Ok during practice.

I went home after the morning class and spent the next hours help-ing Mom in the market or doing errands or chores. In the afternoon I attended another class and then went home to eat dinner and rest. I have never stopped practicing Kuk Sool Won since the day I started when I was fourteen years old. I have only stopped my practice when I have been very sick and after giving birth to my daughters. I have fulfilled my promise to Chief Master.

When I was seventeen years old, Mom moved to Ulsan, a city about two-hours away from Pusan. I decided not to move with Mom, because I did not want to stop my training. It was arranged that I would stay with my sister Choon-Up and Chief Master. I experienced the tradi-tional martial arts training, as it had been done since ancient times, when students lived at the master's home and trained daily. Usually, the do jang was at the master's home, so students had a complete im-mersion not only in their martial arts training, but also in their daily life by sharing meals and a roof with their master. Students training under a master this way agreed to follow their master's instructions and requests twenty-four hours a day, seven days a week, as other fam-ily members did. They left the master's home to visit their family for a short time, but their actual home was where the master lived. This is how I lived until I got married.

I moved to my sister and Chief Master's home and my traditional training began. Besides me, there were four other students living with Chief Master at the time, and one of my sister's responsibilities was to prepare three meals every day for the seven of us and my nieces and nephews. I helped my sister with all the house chores and babysat her children. I helped her cook breakfast, lunch, and dinner; shop for groceries; and help in any other way she asked me to. At the same time, I attended my practice, three times a day.

My routine changed slightly after Mom left for Ulsan. I woke up at the same time, 5:00 a.m., and attended the early morning class that lasted a couple of hours. Then, I returned to my sister and helped her prepare breakfast, tend to the children, and do house chores. By noon, I returned to the do jang for another couple of hours of train-ing before returning to help my sister again. I trained a third time during the two-hour-long night class.

Sometimes I went back to the do jang after everybody had left late at night and practiced for one or two hours more on my techniques. I felt that if I practiced twice as much or maybe ten times more than my classmates, I would be able to perform correctly. Why was this hap-pening to me? The memory of my sister's words came back to me:

Choon-Ok helped her sister Choon-Up care for her little children.

"You're just dumb!" What if they were right? I did not think so; the extra practice was working for me. It didn't matter anyway. I was going to learn all the techniques and forms I had to; I was not going to give it up. I had decided that the option to abandon practice was not available to me. If I abandoned it, I would be breaking my promise to Chief Master and my future would be like it was before I had found Kuk Sool: empty, purposeless, hopeless, and out of my control. Those bleak thoughts put my feet back on the ground. I went back to practice and did not talk about my difficulties to anybody.

I followed this training routine every day. It might sound like a rigid and strenuous schedule to many people; even my friends could not understand how I tolerated such a lifestyle. It was just perfect for me; it was not boring or strenuous at all. This was what I wanted to do. I could fulfill my dream in exchange for helping my sister. It was a very happy period of my life. I was focused on my training. I had no responsibilities other than helping my sister and training as long as I wanted. My dream was coming true. Sometimes, however, I missed Mom and my friends. About every six months I traveled to Ulsan to spend time with Mom and also visit some of my old friends who lived there.

Chapter 13

The Best School

Many people asked me, "Why don't you go to school?"

"My school is Kuk Sool" I replied. "I am not learning martial arts only; I am learning many more things." Chief Master and his brother, our Grand Master Kuk Sa Nim, taught me much more than performing Kuk Sool techniques, forms, weapon use, kicking, and punching. Grand Master is the founder and world leader of Kuk Sool Won and has the title Kuk Sa Nim.

Chief Master In Sun Seo and Kuk Sa Nim In Hyuk Suh gathered the students living with them—sometimes formally, sometimes just in an informal conversation around the dinner table—and talked about their experiences and how they had approached them. By example and by sharing their experiences, they provided lessons that would last a lifetime.

We learned about the dramatic changes Korea was going through at the time, the political turmoil, and how to learn from it without getting into trouble. They provided opposite points of view to give us a balanced perspective about our government struggles, the conflict with North Korea, how Korea was slowly becoming a twentieth-century country, how the United States and other western countries were different from and similar to us, and how they were influencing our way of life. We were exposed in our own do jang to the outside world Chief Master and Kuk Sa Nim had experienced firsthand. It was like being home-schooled.

Our masters were prepared to introduce us to the outside world and teach us how to live in it because they had a good college education and had lived many experiences on their own. They shared their knowledge with us. That is why Kuk Sool was more than a martial arts school. It was a school for life, for a successful life, and this was very important to me. My masters' attitude toward life, especially Kuk Sa Nim's, opened more doors than they closed. Our Grand Master constantly shared his life perspective.

Kuk Sa Nim is living proof that success is hard work combined with patience, optimism, luck, and keeping your feet on the ground. To succeed, you need to believe that you can do more than you think you can. To succeed, you must keep a positive attitude and never give up. You must develop yourself in a positive manner and avoid anything that would affect you negatively. You must educate yourself and focus on what you can do, instead of worrying about what you cannot do. All these beliefs, all these life pillars, are embedded in Kuk Sool training and written down for all students to repeat them and make them their own. I don't think that you can learn such valuable knowledge and life lessons in a textbook in a regular school.

I never thought that Kuk Sool would become part of my personal life, but the two have become one. I learned to ask myself how I would like my life to be, what I would like to accomplish, and what I did not want in my life. I learned to set goals and received guidance to achieve them. If I didn't know how to do something, I found out; I asked somebody who knew. For me, Kuk Sool is the best school there is. It guided me in my journey to achieve the life I wanted to have. It even helped me find my husband.

As time passed and I continued my practice, I liked it more and more and felt empowered by it. I knew deep inside that I would stop my training only if something major happened to me; otherwise, I felt confident that I would be able to keep the promise I made to Chief Master.

When I was about nineteen, I considered the idea of getting married and how I would balance my daily practice with married life, in the traditional Korean style. I watched the other women who practiced in the do jang beside me. Many of them were very, very good at it and dedicated themselves to practice as much as men did. Some of them had received their First Degree Black Belt, others their Second Degree, and some had even made it to the Third Degree Black Belt.

These achievements were not to be taken lightly. Achieving a Third Degree Black Belt represented six to seven years of consistent, regular practice and passing all the necessary tests in front of the Masters to receive the promotion to the next degree. In Kuk Sool Won, students first begin with a white belt and can achieve higher degrees as they progress. Kuk Sa Nim was Chief Master's teacher. Chief Master in a Ninth Degree Black Belt and only Kuk Sa Nim is Tenth Degree Black Belt. The highest level students can attain is Ninth Degree Black Belt. These women were seriously dedicated to studying Kuk Sool, which required hard work and persistence. If it was tough for a man, it demanded even tougher discipline for women living in Korea in the 1970s.

Mom was right; martial arts were not a traditional women's pursuit. Women were supposed to get married, have children, and dedicate their lives to their families, just like my mom and my sisters had done. As my mom had repeated to me many times, "Kuk Sool is not something women do." Actually, times had begun to change in my home country and more and more women became interested in and practiced martial arts. Families were slowly accepting changes in traditional Korean lifestyles. I was hoping I could ride along the slowly emerging modern times and continue with my practice, even after I got married.

I talked to and observed the other women practicing Kuk Sool in our do jang. I was devastated to see that the majority of female students, almost all of them actually, stopped practicing after they got married. They quit because their husbands had told them to stop their practice. Traditional family values persevered and stood their ground in spite of the light breezes of modern times blowing through our society. Old habits are hard to change. I understood that well.

One of the most disappointing times for me occured when a high-ranking woman—I wish I could remember her name—quit after she got married. This lady was a Third Degree Black Belt and very talented. In fact, she had been my inspiration when I started training. She had been in Kuk Sool for many years and I had been very impressed when I saw her and a master performing "Gum Dae Ryun." This is an ancient technique of sword sparring in which one person has a long sword and the other, typically a woman, has two short swords. It is a very difficult technique to master and she was excellent at it. I saw her demonstrate before I began Kuk Sool and my mouth hung open. She was incredible, and I decided at that moment that I wanted to be like her. I thought of her as my role model and knew that one day I wanted to be as good as she was. To my disappointment, marriage forced her to quit forever. Would that happen to me too? What could I do to prevent this?

I did not want to stop practicing Kuk Sool, but I also wanted to get married one day. I was not willing to give up my training; I wanted to continue all my life. Kuk Sool and I were one. Nobody was going to make me stop! If I stopped my practice, it would be for a major reason, maybe health related, but I would not stop just because somebody told me to. I always remembered what Chief Master had told me when I was fourteen years old, begging him to allow me to start practicing. "If you start Kuk Sool, you cannot quit. You have to continue." That was in my mind all the time. How could I continue my practice and at the same time get married and have a family? I had no answer at the time.

In 1974, Kuk Sa Nim left Korea and moved to the United States to establish the World Kuk Sool Association. I became interested in how people lived in the United States. When I went to watch American movies with my friends, I noticed that women's status in America was quite different than in Korea. In traditional Korean families, men and their interests and wishes were always put first, and women's put second. Men made all the family decisions and that was not open for discussion. But the movies I watched and the stories our Masters brought from America were different. In America, men's interests and wishes were not always put first. Many times, women's interests and wishes were put first. Women in America had the opportunity to pursue personal interests separate from the family, and they could play a variety of different roles in society. This was so different from what I was used to.

This idea struck me the first time I heard of it. Women first, men second? I had never thought about that. I had lived in Korea all my life in a traditional family, where the man's wishes were always met first. In my own family, my mother had always placed my father's and her children's needs ahead of hers. She never addressed her own needs. My older sisters and other relatives had followed the same tradition. I guess I assumed that it was the same in any other family anywhere in the world. But the realization that the status of women in society was different in America was a revelation; I had options I had not considered.

One day I was talking to Chief Master, joking. "If I go to the United States, where women are first and men second, then I could do whatever I wanted to do, right? I could continue my practice even if I was married, right?" I said.

"Yes, you could do it," Chief Master replied, looking straight into my eyes.

I laughed.

Even in modern times, thirty years after I was considering my option to move to America, it is very typical that Korean women, in a way, marry not just their husbands, but also their husbands' families. The husband's parents live with their oldest son and their daughter-in-law takes care of them as if they were her own parents. The wife is part of her husband's family and takes care of all the family members, who usually do not understand and accept that women may want to have an interest outside the home, such as Kuk Sool. In America things were different. Women could participate in other activities besides caring for the family, and the family would many times find this acceptable. But, how could I go to the United States?

At first I thought that was an impossible dream. "No, I cannot go to the United States," I thought. I do not speak English. I know almost nothing about that country. I don't know a single person living there. How can I leave Mom alone? It would be unacceptable to my mom and my family for me to live in the United States on my own. A young, single woman cannot even travel by herself in Korea, let alone move to another continent without any family to live with. I did not think it was possible for me to move to America. But, I continued thinking about the possibility. I was determined to continue my practice of Kuk Sool, but it was clear that would not be possible if I had a traditional Korean husband.

When Kuk Sa Nim returned to Korea from the United States, I decided to talk to him about my dilemma. Kuk Sa Nim is the Grand Master of Kuk Sool Won, and he is also Chief Master's brother. Chief Master is my brother-in-law, so I felt that I could approach Kuk Sa Nim with my question. We are family. If we were not related, I would have never asked him to help me.

"Kuk Sa Nim, I want to go to the United States too!" I laughed nervously. "You know that if I marry a Korean man I will have to stop practicing Kuk Sool. I do not want to stop my practice. It is very important to me and I want to continue all my life," I said. "I promised Chief Master I would do so."

Kuk Sa Nim seemed to understand. He nodded his head and looked at me.

"Kuk Sa Nim, do you have any idea how I can go to the United States?" I asked. "I want to continue my training. What if I have a husband who also wants to continue his training? We could train together and I would not have to stop. How can I go to the United States and find an American husband who is committed and practices Kuk Sool as I do?"

Kuk Sa Nim took his time to reply. He looked at his hands while he was thinking of his answer. "I will look for somebody who will be a good match for you and your commitment to Kuk Sool," he replied calmly. "Don't worry about it. You keep training; continue your practice. Leave the husband to me."

"Please, look for my husband. The person you pick for me, I will accept. Whether he is ugly or not, it doesn't matter. If you pick him, I know he is a good man." I laughed nervously at my intense reply.

I trusted Kuk Sa Nim completely, so I put my future in his hands. The man he said would be a good husband for me, I would marry. That was how much trust I placed in Kuk Sa Nim.

"OK. I'll look. Go to your practice," Kuk Sa Nim said, finishing our short conversation about one of the most important issues of my life. I turned around and resumed my practice.

I was not worried at all; on the contrary, I felt that I had taken an important step toward securing my future in Kuk Sool for the rest of my life. Kuk Sa Nim had known me since I was twelve years old. He had seen me as I watched Kuk Sool students practice from far away, because I could not join them. I was playing outdoors all the time; my skin was tanned and shining, my body very thin, and my hair long, silky, and black. He would look at me, touch my head, smile, and say, "This little girl is so cute!" Kuk Sa Nim also knew of my commitment to Kuk Sool practice. I was sure he was going to help me. Kuk Sa Nim returned to the United States. I waited and waited for news from him about my future husband, but for long months, I did not hear anything from him.

Chapter 14

No Cutting in Line

I was twenty years old and a Second Degree Black Belt when Mom came to Pusan and we lived together again for some time. It was a hot and dry summer and we had not had much rain for quite some time. Water supplies were short and we and our neighbors had to rely on the few natural creeks and other water sources still available in the mountain behind our home. Every day, many people went to the mountain with buckets, pots, and pans to collect water for their personal needs, cooking, and cleaning.

At five o'clock one morning, I walked up the trail toward the creek carrying two pails to fill up. There was already a long line of at least twenty people collecting water when I got there. I walked toward the end of the line and waited for my turn. People stayed in line and waited patiently, sometimes starting a conversation with the person in front of or behind them, until their turn arrived. Shortly after I had taken my place at the end of the line, a young, very large man arrived holding two large buckets. He looked very strong. His arms, legs, and chest were muscular; he looked like a wrestler. He approached the long line, walking with heavy, slow steps and looked from the beginning to the end of the line, as if mentally calculating how long it would take him to have his turn to fill his buckets. He sighed and slowly walked to the beginning of the line, and without a word he stepped in front of everybody else, cutting all the people who had been waiting for their turn for more than forty minutes. I could not believe my eyes. "How can he cut? He has to move back to the end, right behind me!" I thought. I dropped my pails on the ground and quickly stepped in his direction.

He was a big young man. Most of the people in line were old men and women, like grandparents. There were not many young men waiting to fill their buckets. It was up to me to ask this young man not to cut in front of all of us; he had to move to the end of the line. I approached him and tapped his shoulder.

"You need to move behind me in the line. I am the last one and these people you cut have been waiting for more than forty minutes," I told him, hands on my hips. He turned slowly in my direction, looked at my face, then turned back, facing the front again, not saying a word. I was getting impatient. I tapped him on the shoulder again, harder. "You need to move behind me in line!" I insisted.

"Be quiet," he said, facing me again. "Go to the end of the line." He turned away from me again.

I stepped in front of him. "You told me to be quiet?" I said, raising my voice and frowning. Everybody in line focused on us. Here was this huge man and this little, thin young woman talking back to him.

"If you don't go back . . . " he said.

"Oh, OK. You want to hit me?" I asked, keeping my head up and my body straight.

"Don't bother me!" he said. "Go to the end of the line."

"*You* better go over there," I replied. "I won't move until you go to the end of the line."

He had had enough of me. He dropped the buckets and raised his hand to hit me, but before he could even swing it in my direction, I hit him hard with a double palm strike on his chest, a move out of the form Cho Geup Hyung. I could not believe what happened. The big man fell hard on his back with a loud *thump*, like a big tree that's just been felled. Everybody was quiet now, looking at us. What was going to happen? He did not get up right away. He continued resting on his back on the hard ground for a few minutes. His eyes were open and looking straight into the still dark skies, dawn barely peaking behind the mountain.

I think he was so shocked that he couldn't understand what had happened to him. Quite probably he had never been pushed to the ground by a person much smaller than him, let alone a small woman. The grandmas and grandpas in line walked toward him and shook their fingers in his face, scolding him.

"Tsk, tsk, tsk," they said. "What happened?" they asked. "We thought you were a very strong man. How come you are so weak that a little woman can put you on the ground with just one strike?" People laughed and returned to their places in line; I went back to the end of the line, too.

He finally stood up clumsily. He recovered his buckets, looked around as if nothing had happened, and walked to the end of the line, standing behind me. He did not say anything to anybody, not even to me. I looked at his face, but he didn't look back. After that incident, I saw him every morning while I waited in line to collect water. He arrived after I did with his two buckets and, without saying a word to me, took his place at the end of the line. One day, he was already in line when I arrived. This time he talked to me.

"Do you want to go in front of me?" he asked.

"No," I replied. "I'll wait for my turn. But don't you forget your manners!"

One day, looking puzzled, he asked me, "How come you have so much power in your little body?".

"I don't have that much power," I said. "You are just weak." He still could not understand. My power was sharply focused, but his was not.

I told Chief Master and the other instructors in the do jang about the incident, and they all laughed at the big man's weakness. Mom did not laugh when I told her. She worried all the time about me getting into fights, because she knew I had a quick temper. "Always be careful," she said. "You are just like me."

Life was not always training, chores, and defending my rights. I also enjoyed a good time with my friends, but I was always scared of my oldest brother's quick temper. Hwa-Nam sometimes hit first and asked questions later. My friends and I were always afraid of his reaction every time we wanted to go to a party. If I told him that I wanted to go to a party with my friends, he would immediately reply, "No. You cannot go anywhere." Hwa-Nam was very protective of me. He took care of my mother and also kept close tabs on me. I needed his permission to go anywhere and do anything except practice Kuk Sool.

My best girl friend insisted that we go to another friend's party that would last all night. "I don't think I can go," I told my friend. "You know my brother. It's impossible."

"OK," said my friend, "I'll tell him we are going to another place, not to a party. You just go along with what I say." I agreed with my friend. The party promised to be very entertaining and I liked to be with my friends, having a good time and playing games.

We talked to Hwa-Nam at my home and my friend told him that we were going to the movies.

"Be back home by 11 o'clock," said my brother. "As soon as the movie finishes, come home."

We agreed and we really thought we could keep our promise and be home by eleven. We would enjoy the party until shortly before eleven and then head home as my brother requested. We would have a wonderful time with friends and keep our promise to my brother. It looked like the perfect plan. We got dressed and headed to my friend's house.

The party was great. My friends were there and there was plenty of food. We played fun games, sang songs, and danced. We were enjoying ourselves so much that we lost track of time and it was past midnight when we noticed how late it was. My best friend and I looked at each other and said, "Forget it! We are having a wonderful time!" We decided to stay at the party, forgetting the promise to my brother. I did not suspect at the time that this decision would have a terrible consequence.

"What are we going to do now?" I asked. There was a curfew between midnight and 4 a.m. We did not want to get shot for walking in the street during curfew time. We could not go back home. If we went home and managed to survive being caught or shot by the soldiers, we reasoned, then my brother would be so mad that he probably would beat us badly. We decided that if we were going to get in trouble anyway, we better enjoy the party some more. We stayed until 4 a.m.

When we arrived home after sunrise, my brother was standing by the door, breathing heavily. My friend and I were so scared that we approached him slowly, heads down, tears dripping from our eyes. My brother walked toward us and slapped my friend hard on the face. She yelped and held her red cheek with one hand, eyes facing the ground.

"I trusted you," said Hwa-Nam. "But not anymore. Never come to my house again!" My friend cried and ran home, leaving me alone with my brother's wrath.

He grabbed me by my collar and pulled me inside the house. I knew I could have done something to defend myself against my brother's anger, but I did not want to do it. He was my brother, and I had been raised to respect him and not to contradict his wishes or actions.

He released all his anger and frustration on me. He slapped me on my back and shoulders. At the same time, he was yelling at me about how he had not been able to sleep all night, waiting for me to get home. He slapped me and I did not defend myself. I moved around the room, trying to avoid his frustration. He told me how worried he had felt all night, not knowing if anything bad had happened to us.

He made me kneel on the floor and smacked the back of my head. I felt terrible pain and cried, but did not defend myself. He was so angry and hitting me so hard that I cried louder and louder. I managed to stand up and walked around the room with my hands together like I was praying, keeping my head down. "I am sorry!" I cried. "I am so sorry!" Then he left the room and closed the door.

I thought he had finished his punishment. I finally could breathe calmly as I continued crying. He came back, slamming the door open and rushing back in. "Oh, no! He's back," I thought, and my body trembled. Punishment was not over yet. Keeping my head down, I raised my eyes high enough to see him. He had a pair of scissors in his hands. What is he going to do? I thought. I panicked.

In two quick steps he stood beside me, grabbed a handful of my waist-long hair and cut it right at scalp level. I was screaming in terror when Mom stepped inside the room with a broom in her hands. I looked up and I saw her frown through my tears. She raised the broom and began hitting my brother hard with the stick. She beat him like a piñata. "Are you crazy?" she yelled to my brother. "How can you cut her hair?"

"I cut her hair so she never lies to us again," replied my brother, raising his arms, trying to shield his body from the broom unsuccessfully. "Remember this!" my brother told me, turning in my direction and shaking my hair in my face. I have never forgotten what he did to my hair. Mom continued hitting him with the broomstick until he ran for the door and left the house.

I was crying quietly now. "Half of my hair is gone! All gone!" I cried, looking at Mom. "Mom, what am I going to do?"

"Don't worry, don't worry," she said in a soothing voice. "Mommy will take care of this. Don't worry." She didn't hit me or punish me in any way. Usually, she would have yelled at me as she always did when I misbehaved, but that day she didn't. I cried and cried most of the day and did not leave the house. The next morning, I did not want to eat. I just cried.

"I cannot go outside anymore," I told Mom. "How am I going to go out on the streets, to practice or to meet my friends looking like this?"

Mom went shopping. She bought five hats, all in a different style, and brought them home for me to try on. I had never worn a hat before, but I decided to try them, and in the mirror they looked cute and pretty. My favorite was a beret. I wore it every day for about three months until my hair was long enough for me not to feel embarrassed in front of other people. I laugh at this now, but at that time I was furious with my brother. I didn't talk to him for a long time; I didn't even look at him. I was mad at him all the time. His punishment made me change my mind about lying to him, though. After that, I always told him where I was really going and I obeyed him. I guess the haircut worked.

When I went to Korea in the late nineties with my husband, I talked to my brother Hwa-Nam, joking about this incident.

"Why did you have to cut my hair that time? Why didn't you leave me alone after all the beating you gave me?" I asked him lightly. "I was a teenager having a good, innocent, fun time at a party. Why did you give such a harsh punishment?" I love my brother and respect him, but I had to tell him. "You didn't have to do that, you know, cut my hair."

He did not answer me. He turned and talked to my husband.

"Barry, you need to buy me a good dinner," he said. "You need to take care of me."

"Why?" asked Barry.

"Because I took good care of your wife when she was young," he said. We all laughed. "I did it so you had a good wife. You need to buy me dinner tonight, because I watched your wife so she wouldn't go out with other guys."

My brother told me that he was always worried about me because I was pretty and he didn't want anything bad to happen to me, like it had happened when I was nine years old. I understand that my brother felt compelled to protect me, but why cut my hair so short?

My brother has a temper, but he has fulfilled his son's duties well, following Korean family traditions. He took good care of Mom when she could not care for herself. He and his wife stayed in Korea all their lives and cared for Mom until she passed away in 2001. I will always be thankful to my brother and sister-in-law for taking care of her.

I remember when I complained to Mom about her favoring my brothers over me and my sisters. When we had little food, she served them the best pieces. When we were eating, she served them first, and my sisters and I ate after my brothers had eaten. When my brothers earned money, she asked for part of it, but when I earned money, Mom asked me to give her all of it. This made me angry. "Why are they your favorites?" I asked her. "I help you around the house more than they do. I give you all my money. I am your daughter! Why do you treat them better than you treat me?"

"According to our traditions, it is your oldest brother who will take care of me when I am old," Mom said. "You and your sisters will not care for me because after you get married you will become part of your husband's family, assuming your daughter-in-law responsibilities, which include caring for your husband's parents. You will not care for me when I am old; your brother will. I have to take good care of him now and even give him preference so he takes good care of me when I am old and I need him to." That is a tradition many Korean families follow even today. Some traditions have been lost, but the way parents are cared for has stayed the same.

I have found you a husband

Kuk Sa Nim spoke to Chief Master on the phone often. Once he told Chief Master "I have three American students," Kuk Sa Nim said. "I am observing them closely. One might be a good husband for Choon-Ok, but I don't know which one yet."

That's all I heard. No details about their looks or their personality. Were they tall like most Americans I had seen in the movies? What color was their hair? Were they handsome, strong, skinny? Were their voices soft or loud? Many Americans spoke loud. I had to work on my patience. It would have been unacceptable to ask Kuk Sa Nim anything about his three American students. It would have been considered very rude if I had asked him; it would have implied that I did not trust his judgment. I did not ask anything at all and waited for him to tell me when he had found my husband. I trusted Kuk Sa Nim completely. I had to focus on my practice and forget about my future husband. One thing was certain; I did not have a boring life.

My girl friends knew that I practiced Kuk Sool and that I knew how to take care of myself, and they wanted me to take care of them, too. Every time they wanted to go out to the movies, or to have tea or coffee, they invited me to go with them. They knew they would be safe with me. "Can you go with us?" they asked me.

"OK, let's go to the movies," I said. We liked to watch a variety of movies. I remember *Gone with the Wind, Cleopatra,* the James Bond movies, *Rocky,* and *Grease,* just to mention a few.

We were at the movies one time, waiting in our seats for the movie to begin, when my friend Young-Ja, who was sitting beside me, tapped my arm and told me that there was a young man sitting next to her making her a little nervous. The movie began and only a few minutes had passed when my friend touched my arm and whispered, "Look!" I looked toward the man sitting next to her and saw his hand slowly moving toward her thigh, then resting it on top of her leg. My friend removed the young man's hand from her thigh, placing it on his thigh. He waited a few seconds, then moved his hand again and rested it on my friend's thigh. He didn't say a word; he pretended he was watching the movie with a grin on his face, but it was obvious that he wanted to feel her body.

"What can I do? What can I do? He keeps putting his hand on my leg!" my friend whispered into my ear. I could see that she was about to cry. I always felt anger first, when most girls felt fear, but I stayed calm.

"Do you want to switch seats with me?" I asked her. We switched, and I was now sitting next to the young man. He turned and looked at me. I looked back at him and smiled.

A few minutes later, he slowly rested his hand on my thigh. I removed his hand slowly, and put it back on his thigh. He persisted, putting his hand on my thigh one more time. I looked at him and smiled. I turned back and pretended to watch the movie. Without a word, I drew back my elbow and hit him hard in the middle of his chest, right on the solar plexus, knocking his wind out. He gagged and bent over, trying to catch his breath. I hit him on the back of his neck with the edge of my hand, using "sudo" or knife-hand strike, and he fell to the floor, gasping for air.

Everybody around us stood up and looked in the direction of his strange noises. Nobody knew what had happened in the darkness of the movie theatre. There was plenty of confusion and loud voices and gasping-for-air noises mixed with the movie soundtrack. The young man was out of breath and kneeling on the floor, trying to recover. People yelled, "What happened? What has happened?" After a few minutes, people calmed down. The young man stood up and left, holding his arms around his chest without uttering another word. He didn't even look at me. He just left. The audience sat back in their seats and slowly quieted down. We all continued watching the movie as if nothing had happened.

My friend Young-Ja whispered, "That was better than the movie!"

We laughed, people hushed us, and I whispered back to her, joking, "Next time we go somewhere together and I help you like today, you have to pay me."

The next time my friends and I went out we had another confrontation. Two of my friends, Young-Ja and Un-Ok, and I were walking to the coffee shop on very wet streets. It had been raining earlier and we had to walk around many muddy puddles. In those days, Pusan had many unpaved streets that became very muddy and messy when it rained.

Down the street, right ahead of us, a couple of young men were walking in our direction. As they approached us, we could see that they were talking to each other and looking at us, laughing. I had the feeling that those men were not going to pass beside us without causing trouble. My friends were worried. "What can we do? What can we do?" they whispered nervously. "Should we turn around?"

"Don't worry," I told them. "Let's continue walking in a single line. I'll go first." We made a single line and walked forward while the two men also continued on their path directly toward us. They had no doubt that we would move away from their path as soon as we got close, because it was customary that girls had to yield to boys. But not this time. My friends walked behind me, following my quick straight pace. I was not going to yield. The young men got closer and closer to us and as the first one got very close, he opened his arm as if he wanted to hug me. I said to myself, "He doesn't have any idea what I am going to do."

Young-Ja said, "Choon-Ok, please be careful."

I hit the first man hard on his chest with my shoulder. I had practiced this technique regularly during training, but this was the first time I had the occasion to use it for real. And it worked. He fell right in a mud puddle. The other man beside him jumped back quickly, avoiding most of the splatter. We laughed with all our hearts. Young-Ja also jumped back and said, "Yeah, Choon-Ok! You got another one!" It was a very funny sight. We did not stick around; we continued walking quickly toward the coffee shop, leaving the two men wondering what had happened. We heard them talking as we walked away.

"What happened to you?" asked the standing man.

The man sitting in the mud puddle looked at him, puzzled. "I don't know how I ended up in the mud," he replied, clearly confused. "I don't know what she did to me!"

"You are so stupid! Stand up and let's go before someone sees you," his friend said.

I recall one more occasion in which I had to step up and defend myself and my friends. This time it was in a night club. I was in Ulsan visiting my mom when I took the opportunity to meet some friends. We were at a friend's house, chatting, listening to music, and dancing around the room to a Monkeys song playing on the radio. Then, one of my friends had an idea: "Why don't we go to a real night club?"

"That's a great idea!" everyone shouted in unison, and we left.

It was very crowded at the night club, but soon the waiter had a table for us. We put our purses down at the table and rushed out to the dance floor, screaming and yelling like we were at the beach. We were having a great time and nobody paid any attention to us; the music was so loud that it blended in with our screams. We were dancing with each other, but before long some guys tried to dance with us. There was one young man who was particularly persistent, but we did not want to dance with him or any other guy. We had come to dance together. We did not want any trouble.

My friends kept pushing me in front of them toward the man while he insisted we dance with him. Despite my rejections, he continued to bother me and suddenly he grabbed the inside of my wrist and pulled me towards him. I automatically counter-grabbed the inside of his wrist and with the other hand I grabbed his elbow, spun under his arm, folding it tight, and pulled him down hard, a technique called Ki Bohn Soo number three.

The man hit the wooden dance floor flat on his back with a thud and his head bounced off the floor like a basketball. I had his arm folded up and I put my knee on the back of his arm, pinning it with all my weight. He screamed from the pressure on his arm. I wasn't angry, so I released his arm and I helped him to his feet with a smile. He looked at me in surprise and asked, "How did you do that to me?"

I responded simply, "Don't touch me!"

He took a step back, put both hands up and said, "OK, *no problem!*"

I continued dancing with my friends and the young man went back to dancing with his friends. Of course his friends were doubled over with laughter at what had happened to him. It was a great night of fun for everyone after that.

During the time I lived in Pusan with my sister and Chief Master, I had a few more encounters with young men who openly dared to bully and disrespect women, and in each instance I felt compelled to stand up for myself and others and did not tolerate the bullying. I got into trouble for that, as Mom always feared I would, but in my mind there was nothing else I could do. Women should not have to tolerate any type of bullying or disrespect from anybody. Kuk Sool not only taught me patience, but also how to defend myself if I had to.

From time to time I thought about what my future husband would look like. I was always paying attention to Chief Master when he mentioned Kuk Sa Nim. I wanted to know if he was coming to Korea soon. Maybe he would bring me news about my husband-to-be. I knew he would find me a good match. One year after I had talked to Kuk Sa Nim, he sent me a message through Chief Master, "I have found you a husband."

I was surprised. I did not ask any questions; I just looked at Chief Master.

He continued, "We will have a demonstration of Kuk Sool in Hawaii to celebrate the seventy-fifth Anniversary of the Koreans' emigration to Hawaii. Kuk Sa Nim wants you to be in the demo team and he will send your future husband there, too. Kuk Sa Nim will be there and make the introductions."

I couldn't wait to go to Hawaii! Maybe I could demo with him? I arrived in Hawaii and looked for Kuk Sa Nim. My future husband would be close by. I found Kuk Sa Nim, but he had not brought any American students with him. I dared to ask, "How come you did not bring my husband?"

"There were problems. He couldn't make it," he replied. I was very disappointed. I learned later that Kuk Sa Nim had not talked about me to my future husband yet, because he had not decided if he was right for me. I went back to Korea after the demo to continue my practice and waited. I was not interested in anybody else at the time; however, Master K was interested in me.

He was one of Chief Master's students and instructors at the school. He was an excellent martial artist. He invited me to have coffee after practice one day and we talked about practice and how much we liked it. He wanted to go out more, but I was not interested. I had other plans.

Chapter 15

Finding My Power

I was disappointed when I could not meet my future husband in Hawaii, but there was nothing I could do except focus on my training. I think this was good for me, because there was one issue that had been bothering me. In spite of all my practice, I could not get it right. It just didn't look the same as when Chief Master or the other instructors did it. I had not learned to knock down an opponent with a single punch. All the male instructors had the power to do it, and they laughed at me when I tried but did not achieve the expected result. I had power in my fist, but not enough to knock the opponent down with one strike.

I knew I had power in me. I had brought the big, young wrestler who had cut in the water line to the ground with just one double-palm strike. I must not have been doing it quite right with my punches. They were not effective at disabling other people. I observed Chief Master when he practiced on the punching bag. I observed the other instructors too, and then I practiced. But, though I had been able to learn other skills with precision, even though it had always taken me much more practice than other Black Belts, the "one-punch-down" was elusive. I was frustrated.

In my Kuk Sool school today, students are free, even welcome, to ask me or another instructor for help when they have difficulties learning a skill. This was not so during my time as a student. Traditional Kuk Sool and other martial arts teaching does not accept that students might need to ask their instructors for more instruction. This is considered disrespectful to the Master because by asking him to teach you something, you are implying that he does not know how to instruct you. Some students have been removed from a school permanently for asking for new instruction. So I did not ask. I practiced my punches when Chief Master was on the practice floor and hoped that he would notice that I was having difficulties. He didn't.

I was very frustrated one day, after long hours of practicing on the punching bag, tolerating the jokes of my fellow instructors about the lack of power in my punches. I had also practiced punching a plain piece of paper to develop fast and light punches. That would give me precision, accuracy, and, most importantly, speed. I had to try to punch the paper so fast and lightly that it wouldn't move. Still, in spite of intense and long practice, I felt that my punches were not effective. They were weak.

When I went home to help my sister with chores, I blurted out all my frustration as soon as Chief Master was in the room with us. I told her in a clear and easily overheard voice how bad I felt because, in spite of all my constant practice, my punches were not powerful enough to knock an opponent down in a single attempt. I wanted to learn to do it. It was important for my training. I had practiced so much with the paper and the bags, but I still did not manage to punch effectively. Maybe I needed a real-life experience to learn to punch with knock-down power. I was sure Chief Master could hear me. I talked to my sister; I did not address Chief Master directly, but he could hear me clearly. I was not asking Chief Master to teach me, but he was now aware of my need indirectly. He did not say a word. My sister prepared dinner and I helped her and repeated my desire to learn "one-punch-down" strikes.

A few days later, my sister and I went grocery shopping together and, on our way back home, an intoxicated young man followed us. He got close enough that we could hear his inappropriate remarks about us. I don't recall exactly what he was saying, but it was enough for my sister to pick up the pace and urge me to walk faster, too. My sister was nervous and continued increasing her speed. I was feeling angry. I waited a few minutes for the man to go away on his own after we did not reply to his intrusion, but he continued following us in a zig-zag path, catching up with our pace.

I could not wait any longer. "Do you want me to do something about him?" I asked Choon-Up, for her ears only.

"No. Keep walking fast. I don't want any street trouble," she replied. Her voice was shaking. I could not tolerate any more of the man's foul language and disrespect. I stopped dead in my path, turned, and looked at him.

"Why are you following us?" I demanded.

"Oh, you two girls look so good!" he said, slurring his words. His body swayed left to right as he tried to steady his feet on the ground.

He had a stupid grin on his face, his eyes were red, and he held his pants with one hand.

"Really?" I said. "Do you want to come to our house with us?"

"Oh, yeah!" His eyes opened a bit more and his smile widened. "Wherever you go, I'll go with you!"

"OK, follow us," I replied. My sister looked at me, wondering what I was going to do. "Let's go," I told her.

The man followed us to the do jang, which was on the second floor of a four-story building. Our living quarters were on the other floors. When we arrived, I told him, "Wait here. We are going to drop our shopping bags and then I'll come back to take you to our home."

"OK!" he said, still grinning.

My sister and I climbed the stairs quickly. She disappeared into the kitchen and I went directly to the practice floor of the do jang. There were no students at the time; only the instructors were practicing. Chief Master was also present, and I told him about the annoying, intoxicated man waiting downstairs, how he had followed us all the way home from the market, and how he had been bothering us continuously with his foul language and indecent suggestions.

"I kept telling him to stop bothering us, but he persisted and now he is downstairs waiting," I explained to Chief Master and the other instructors who had come closer to hear the story. Chief Master crossed his arms on his chest and thought about it for a minute or two.

"Bring him upstairs," he commanded the male instructors. Five of them ran downstairs and dragged the man to the practice floor. He was not smiling anymore.

Chief Master looked at me. "I want you to do what I am going to tell you," he told me.

"What do I need to do?" I replied, nervously, unsure of what his request would be.

"You are going to practice knock-down punches now," he said.

I was surprised. He had definitely heard me when I had complained to my sister about my frustration at not mastering the punches, and he was using this situation to teach me how to do it. This was real-life training. Chief Master had given an order, so I had to do it.

By now, the young man was almost sober after realizing the kind of trouble he had gotten himself into. He attempted to run away, but two instructors held him by the arms tightly as he was screaming, "Let me go!" But he could not go anywhere.

Chief Master looked at me and said, "Punching practice: right now."

"But, can I do this?" I asked. "He's not a punching bag."

"Yes, you can do this, no problem," replied Chief Master, matter-of-factly. "Now is a good chance to practice."

I approached the screaming young man slowly. I set my stances to punch and hit him in the stomach with all my strength. The drunken man bent over a little, releasing his breath. When he straightened his body, he was just laughing at me. I could not believe it! Even an intoxicated stranger laughed at my punches. I punched him two, three, four times, but he just tightened his muscles, released his breath with every strike, and laughed in my face.

I turned to Chief Master. "How can I do it?" I asked, frustrated. "I keep punching and punching but he just laughs!"

"More practice," said Chief Master calmly. "Look at me." He approached the young man and punched him hard on the side of the jaw. He fell unconscious on the floor. One punch and he was down. No more laughing. As I later found out, Chief Master had hit him with only a fraction of his power. He had not broken the man's jaw or teeth. He had very precisely knocked him out without extra damage, demonstrating the extraordinary control of a true master. I was amazed at this amount of power and precise control.

The instructors picked him up and dragged him all the way to the police station nearby. He spent the night there and was free the next day, sober and confused, probably unsure about what had happened. I am sure he had not had an experience like this one before. I had never done something like this before either. It was not going to be the only time. I had tried, but I had not learned the knock-down punch yet.

Chief Master knew that I had not learned to punch as well as I had wanted to. I looked unhappy for days after the experience, but did not say a word to him. He asked me, "Why are you upset?"

"I am so weak!" I said. "My punches are so weak!"

"Sit by the window and watch the street," he said, pointing at the do jang's wide windows. "When you see a man doing something bad on the street, call me."

I watched the street all afternoon, but nothing unusual happened for a long time. It was night when I saw the shadow of a man walking toward our school, swaying right and left, definitely drunk. He steadied his stances and urinated on the wall next to the do jang door. I called Chief Master and he sent four instructors downstairs to carry the drunk to the do jang. He was screaming, "What are you doing?" in not-so-nice language and trying to free himself from the instructors' grip, but he had no luck. "What did I do?" he asked many times. Two instructors held the man by his arms, forcing him to stay still.

"Punching practice right now," said Chief Master, looking at me.

This time I knew where to hit. I did not aim for the stomach. I hit the jaw with my fist as hard as I would hit the punching bag. This time I knocked him out. This time I got it right. I was surprised at myself and I looked at my fist in amazement. It wasn't hurting; the skin wasn't broken or anything. I had done it and I was fine. The other instructors took him to the police station for him to sleep overnight in jail and to be released in the morning. I had successfully delivered my first knock-down punch. Patience, perseverance, and practice had paid off.

Real-life punching practice is now illegal in Korea; people could go to jail for that or for any kind of hitting or kicking. But in the 1970s, real-life training like this was not punished with jail time. It was considered assistance to the police's efforts to keep the streets clean of unruly drunks. Those were different times and now things are done in a different way, but that was how things were done when I was training.

Chapter 16

Mom Said No!

Chief Master came to my home with a message from Kuk Sa Nim; Kuk Sa Nim had found a good husband for me and asked if it would be possible for us to start writing each other. Mom said no. "No, you cannot do that; you cannot marry a man who is not Korean. I do not want you to marry an American man." And so she repeated for a whole year. I tried many times to change her mind. She still said no.

I had to wait again. I could not write or receive letters from my future husband without Mom's consent. Chief Master nodded and left. I talked to him about this and he said we had to wait until Mom approved of us writing each other letters.

"Go practice and be patient," he said.

Perhaps Master K thought I might reconsider his invitations now that Mom had not approved an American husband. He asked me to have coffee with him after practice again. I accepted; it was friendly talk for me. He talked differently this time.

"So you are looking for an American husband?" he said.

"I asked Kuk Sa Nim to help me find one," I said.

"Korean men are good husbands, you know. You are a Korean woman; you should marry a Korean man," he said.

"In America, I can continue my training," I said.

"How far do you think you can get? Training is not easy; it gets harder as you advance. Women are not as tough as men. Leave martial arts to men," Master K said.

"This is a private matter," I said and left the coffee shop.

My heart was racing and my face felt hot. I couldn't believe that I had waited so long for Kuk Sa Nim to find me an American husband and now Mom had denied me the chance to start our "mail dating." There was nothing I could do. This issue was bigger than others Mom had been opposed to. This was not only about having a husband who was not one of us; it meant leaving Korea and moving to a country where we did not have any relatives or friends. I could not see a solution to this problem at that time. I continued my practice intensely and had a few more real street-fight experiences that proved to me that Kuk Sool was the best school for me.

It was my birthday, February 16, and a very cold day. My sister and Chief Master invited me to lunch to celebrate; we went out to a good restaurant. We walked through narrow streets filled with side-by-side steaming food stands displaying a large variety of foods from soups to fried or steamed vegetables and meats. The street was crowded with people, and it was loud with the chopping and stirring of foods and the voices of the merchants announcing their goods. They all cooked and sold their food right at their stands, cutting and chopping vegetables and meats with long, sharp knives.

We were walking through the street, my sister and Chief Master together in front, and me following a few steps behind them. I was mesmerized by all the noises, smells, and the wonderful food; I lagged behind my family. In one of the stands, I saw that two young men were playing with large cutting knives. They saw me, stopped playing with the knives, and stared at me. I ignored them; I kept walking, following my sister and Chief Master from a distance and enjoying the busy street. All of a sudden, I saw a knife coming straight toward the front of my body. Automatically, I defended myself against the attack with "Dahn Do Maki," a self-defense technique against knife attacks. I secured the attacker's wrist with both my hands, and twisted it to one side. The young man screamed and fell to the ground.

Chief Master heard the scream and turned around very quickly to see what had happened behind his back. Immediately, he saw the young man with a knife in his hand getting up from the ground. Chief Master ran toward him and hit him on the chest with a flying side kick. This time, the young man did not get up from the ground so quickly. Chief Master moved toward the other young man. He was not armed but still wanted to fight.

I don't remember exactly how Chief Master got both of them into the double wrist lock; it was so fast I could barely see it.

"Come here, you!" said Chief Master as he grabbed one of the men. He held the man's wrist with one hand, and the other man's wrist with his other hand, locking their wrist joints.

"Why are you arresting me? I didn't do anything!" squealed one of the men. I could not believe how loud those men screamed as Chief Master put pressure on their wrists. They screamed all the way to the police station nearby, as Chief Master dragged them through the street. My sister Choon-Up just looked at me and her husband, rolled her eyes, and shook her head in exasperation.

Choon-Up and I followed Chief Master to the police station, where everybody wondered what had happened. I told the police that the young man had attacked me with a knife and that I had defended myself.

"You disarmed this man?" the police officer asked incredulously.

"I did," I replied. "Can I go now? I want to go and have lunch."

The police were very surprised that a young woman like me could defend herself against a knife attack like I had just done. They looked at each other shaking their heads; they could not believe a woman could do this kind of thing.

The two men went to jail and I went to have lunch with my sister and Chief Master as we had planned. My sister was now very upset.

"I will never take you out to lunch again. You are so much trouble," she said to me.

"I did not do anything," I protested. "The man with the knife attacked me first; I just defended myself."

Chief Master was not upset at all. "Oh, she's no problem," he told my sister, smiling. We enjoyed lunch together without mentioning the incident again, but I still could not believe that my sister thought I was so much trouble.

My life revolved around my daily training and helping my sister with chores. It was very cold during the winter, so I was thankful to have three daily practices at the do jang as well as my duties teaching students, because the exercise kept me warm. During summer time, we had the opportunity to enjoy the beach, which was about a one-hour drive from the school. This gave us a break from the very hot weather, which made practice harder and more draining.

One very hot summer day we went to the beach in Pusan. Chief Master decided that my sister, my brother, five other instructors, and I would go with him to enjoy a day at Haeundae Beach. There were so many people on the beach that you could barely move around. There were people swimming and bathing in the cold sea, sitting on the warm sand, and running or playing on the shoreline. There were men, women, and children. It seemed that everybody living in Pusan had decided to come to the beach.

I did not swim, but I stayed in the shallow water, keeping cool. The day passed quickly and soon it was late afternoon and time to go home. After I had changed my clothes, I was standing on the boardwalk just above the beach level, looking at the crowd that still refused to leave the cool water and refreshing breeze.

Two young men were walking in my direction, talking to each other and looking at me, smiling. I wasn't looking at them; I was aware of them coming, but my attention was captured by the crowd of people on the beach. When one of the men walked by me, he grabbed my breast with one of his hands quickly, then he

Choon-Ok at Haeundae Beach, the day of the big fight.

laughed and both of them ran away. I was stunned. I could not believe he had done that! I looked at them; they were jogging away, laughing and shaking hands. I sprang toward them.

Choon-Ok at Haeundae Beach, before the big fight.

I reached the first man quickly, pulled him around by his shirt toward me and punched him. Blood splashed his face. He grabbed his nose and screamed. Then I felt my hair being pulled back harshly. The other young man had wrapped my waist-long, loose hair around his arm and pulled it. The three of us fell to the ground and rolled to the edge of the boardwalk above the beach. We fell down off the boardwalk onto the sand; it was probably a six-foot drop. The three of us yelled in pain, but we did not let go of each other.

I do not remember what I was trying to do to defend myself. It was a tangle of punches and kicks, but there was not much else I could do because one of the men still had my hair wrapped tight around his arm, almost immobilizing me. The pain was sharp on my neck, hair, and head, but I could not stop and let them get away with it. I continued kicking and punching, and I tried to block the men's punches and kicks. A crowd began to surround us to watch the fight, screaming words I could not understand. I was focused on blocking their attacks and trying to land as many blows as I could. I had no idea how to free my hair from the man's arm in order to better defend myself. I continued kicking and punching for what seemed like a very long time.

At the same time, my sister was looking for me to go home. She saw a commotion far away; a large circle of people watching what seemed like a fight. Chief Master said, "Let's see what kind of fight is going on over there." He didn't know it was me.

My sister reached the circle of people first and pushed her way through. At first, she saw two men and a young woman wrestling on the sand furiously; there was plenty of screaming, punching, and kicking. The young woman had her hair wrapped around one man's arm and her head was being pulled right and left, back and forth. My sister's face froze.

"It's my sister!" she screamed. "This is my sister!" She sprinted toward us and joined the fight. She seized the forearm of the man who had control of my hair and screamed, "Let her go!"

The man ignored her. Choon-Up was desperate to help me, so she bit his forearm as hard as she could. She bit him so hard that some of his skin got stuck between her teeth. The man screamed in pain, but still he did not let go of me.

Chief Master and the other instructors joined the crowd and realized what was going on. My sister stepped back from the fight and my fellow instructors joined in, knee-kicking and elbowing the two men. One of the men managed to get up and ran away through the screaming crowd, but the one who had control of my hair was trapped with me, kicking and punching on the sand. Finally, the man released my hair and ran away through the mass of people watching us.

"Go catch them!" Chief Master ordered the instructors. The instructors cut through the crowd and looked for the young men unsuccessfully. There were still so many people on the beach that it was easy for the young men to blend in and hide. Chief Master was very angry when he realized that he might not be able to capture them. "We are not going home tonight until we find those two men!" he commanded.

My sister was worried about me. "Are you OK?" she asked me many times. My hair and my neck were hurting so much that I had to rub them with both hands to try to ease the pain.

"What happened?" my sister asked. "How did the fight begin?"

"One of the men grabbed my breast . . . " I began to tell her.

"That was all? Grabbing your breast is OK," my sister said matter-of-factly. "Why did you make so much trouble because of that?"

"No, it's not *OK*. Nobody touches me where I don't want them to!" I told her firmly. "He cannot do that to me; he made me angry. I could not let him go like nothing had happened."

"You are always so much trouble!" my sister snapped. "Next time we come to the beach, you stay home. You need to be more patient; you get mad too fast." I could not understand my sister.

"If somebody does something to me I do not agree with, I have to let them know I do not approve of their actions," I said, looking her in the eye. "This is how I lead my life, sister. If I think something is not right, I will try to straighten it out, to make it clear that I disagree with their actions. I will not back down. If I have to fight, I will!"

Many times, men think that Korean women are weak. I grew up seeing men place their interests and needs first. It is how we are brought up in the family and what Confucian philosophy teaches. But many young men bother young, pretty women in the street. Many girls and women have gone through what I experienced when I was only nine years old. This marks girls permanently. I know. I had told myself years ago that nobody was going to hurt me and make me cry anymore. Nobody would touch me where I didn't want them to, and if someone did touch me, I would teach him a lesson so he would not do it again. Nobody was going to make me cry.

"We are not going home tonight until we catch those men!" repeated Chief Master when the instructors returned empty-handed. We stayed on the beach until nearly nine o'clock, wondering where the two young men might be. Maybe they had already left the beach and gone home. But there was still a chance that they were hiding on the beach, waiting for us to give up and leave. One of the instructors approached Chief Master with good news.

"I think I have found them," he said. "I heard two men talking a few steps from here. One of them was saying, 'I think we have made a big mistake.' The other one said, 'But you are the one who dared me to grab the girl's breast. You said you would buy me dinner if I did it!'"

The men had not expected what had happened. They had not expected that a young girl would chase them and fight them for their behavior. Every time they had done this before, young girls just let them go like nothing had happened. They had gotten away with it every time before. Not this time.

It had to be them. Chief Master, my five fellow instructors, my sister, and I walked silently to where the young men were hiding and surrounded them. They could not get away this time. "We have bad luck today!" the two young men said when they saw us blocking their escape. All the instructors closed in on them and punched them a few times when they tried to escape. They held them tight by their arms and took them to the police station. They did not protest or offer any more resistance. Maybe they had had enough fighting for one day. We could now go home and rest.

Ah, my temper . . . My quick temper. I had to be aware of it. Controlling my first impulse has always been one of the hardest things for me to do. When something or someone threatens me or a member of my family, I get angry, react, and then think about it later. Mom was always worried this would get me into serious trouble one day. She warned me many times. One of those occasions happened at night when I was about seventeen or eighteen years old.

My oldest sister, Choon-Ja, had asked me to spend the night at her home, which was a one-room house with another room for the kitchen, to watch over her place because she would be out the entire night. My sister was concerned that thieves in the area might rob her home if nobody watched it. If somebody stayed home, thieves might be discouraged to come and rob the house and look for an empty one instead. I agreed to stay in her home. When my sister left, I spent the evening listening to the radio and reading. Before I went to sleep, I ate an apple and left the knife beside my pillow. I fell asleep without noticing I had forgotten to lock the door.

Around 2:30 in the morning, I woke up, startled. I felt very cold and had a strange feeling that something was wrong. I opened my eyes, but instead of the ceiling, I saw the face of a big man standing over me, looking down at me. My heart almost stopped.

I bolted upright and looked around. My reaction startled the man and he jumped back towards the door. I saw the knife I had used to slice the apple and grabbed it quickly. When he saw the knife in my hand, he ran out the door, away from the house. I ran after him, yelling as loud as I could, "Doh-duk-e-yahhh! Doh-duk-e-yahhh!" which means thief in Korean. I chased him for a while and then stopped in my tracks. "What am I doing?" I asked myself. It was so dark I couldn't see anything. I had run out of the house, chasing a strange man, and there I was, standing in the dark with no shoes and a knife in my hand. I panicked. I froze in my tracks. I tried to turn around to go back, but I was so scared I did not move. Why had I run after him? What was I thinking?

I felt like someone was going to grab me at any moment. I walked backwards toward the house very slowly, step by step, looking right and left in case somebody was coming to get me. After several steps, I turned around and ran back to my sister's home. I slammed the door shut behind me. About ten minutes later, I heard someone coming towards the door. The thief was back. "What can I do?" I thought. I answered myself quickly: "I can fight!" With the knife in my hand, I kicked the door open, but no one was there. "He must be hiding," I thought. Then I saw the thief's shoes in front of the door. He was coming back for his shoes. I grabbed the shoes and threw them into the darkness as far as I could. "Don't come back!" I called. I locked the door and sat on the bed, but I could not sleep.

When Choon-Ja returned home near sunrise, I was very much awake. After I told her what had happened, she said, "Are you crazy? Why did you follow the thief? You might have been hurt! And it's curfew time! The soldiers could have found you running in the street with a knife in your hands and they might have shot you right there in front of my house!"

I knew my sister was right. I had acted before thinking.

My sister continued, "Next time do not yell 'Thief!' because people will not come to help you. But, if you yell, 'Fire!' most of our neighbors will come out of their homes to help."

I told my sister I thought the thief had taken something that belonged to her and wanted to get it back. It was my responsibility to take care of Choon-Ja's place.

I told my mom. She was worried again. "That's a big problem with your personality," she said. "It's just like mine, because we don't always think first. We act without thinking and sometimes that can get us hurt. It has taken me a long time to learn to think first and act later."

I wondered if I would ever learn to think first and then act.

Chapter 17

Mom's Change of Heart

In time my sister Choon-Up and Chief Master decided to move to the United States too, following Kuk Sa Nim. When they began to make arrangements to move to the United States with their family, I wondered what would happen to me. Chief Master was convinced by now of my commitment to Kuk Sool practice. He must have thought about my bleak future in Kuk Sool if I stayed in Korea and eventually married a Korean man. He knew that might mean the end of my Kuk Sool career. On the other hand, if I moved to the United States, other options would open for me and I might be able to continue my career as a martial artist and as a married woman. Kuk Sa Nim had already found me a husband. Chief Master talked to my mom.

"If Choon-Up and I go to the United States, Choon-Ok can come with us and we will take care of her as we do here. She won't be going by herself; family will be there supporting her, just as we have supported her here in Korea," said Chief Master.

"If you go to the United Sates with your family," Mom told Chief Master, "then Choon-Ok can go. She can now receive letters from the American."

Mom had said yes! One year after I had asked her permission to "date" an American man, she said yes. I could hardly believe it, but it was true. I was going to marry an American man.

Master K walked with me as I left the do jang. He brought up the topic of my American husband again.

"I heard about your American, the one you want to marry," he said.

"So?" I said.

"I heard he has a very pretty blond girlfriend in America as we speak," he said, smiling.

"Good," I said. "We have not even met yet. We don't know what's going to happen. He's not engaged to me."

"You should look around more. There are good Korean men who also practice Kuk Sool. You are a Korean woman; you should marry a Korean man," he said.

"This is my problem," I said, and left for home.

My American husband-to-be and I began writing each other. We wrote letters back and forth between Korea and the United States for a year. His name is Barry Harmon. When we first started writing, we were both Third Degree Black Belts.

I think that we were meant to be together as husband and wife. I learned much later that Barry had already expressed his interest in marrying me to Kuk Sa Nim before the Grand Master had mentioned me to him. Barry did not go to the Kuk Sool demonstration in commemoration of the Sevety-fifth Anniversary of Korean Emigration to Hawaii, but later he saw the poster made for that occasion. My picture was in the poster and when Barry saw it, he told me years later, it captured his interest. Barry approached Kuk Sa Nim and asked him if he could arrange for us to meet or begin contact somehow. Kuk Sa Nim said, "I'll think about it," and that was it.

At the time, my future husband was a Kuk Sool student practicing the traditional Korean way. He was living and practicing with Kuk Sa Nim in his school in San Francisco, California. At the same time, I was also a traditional Kuk Sool student in Pusan, living and training in Chief Master's school. It seems to me that our marriage being arranged the traditional Korean way was a natural consequence of the way we were living and training. In our case, Kuk Sa Nim made the match that began our relationship in 1979, which still continues today.

It had been a year since Barry had asked Kuk Sa Nim to arrange our meeting. He thought Kuk Sa Nim had forgotten about it, but he did not dare to ask. He knew that it was not proper to ask, because he had asked his master to do something for him. Regardless of how long it might take, students must be patient and wait until their master gives his answer. That is the traditional Korean way. We followed the tradition and exercised our patience. After about a year, Kuk Sa Nim said to Barry, "OK. You can start writing to her." That was it. Barry was surprised, because the subject had not been mentioned for so long.

Writing to each other was not easy, and it was mostly not a private matter. Nevertheless, we wrote each other letters to get to know one another. It was embarrassing sometimes.

At that time, Barry did not speak or write Korean, and I did not speak any English. Barry wrote his letters in English and Chief Master translated them for me, and I wrote my letters in Korean and Kuk Sa Nim translated for Barry. It was not so bad for Barry because Kuk Sa Nim translated my letters in the privacy of his office. He did it in private, because Barry was a senior instructor at Kuk Sa Nim's school. This was not the case for me.

Now that I think about it, it was very funny. Every time we had mail, the mailman brought it to the top floor of the do jang, all the way up, stepping loudly on the wooden steps, *pom, pom, pom.* I could hear him coming up the stairs. I looked at him as he got the mail out of his bag. We could tell if there was mail from the United States by just looking at the envelopes, because they looked different from Korean mail. Korean mail was in plain white envelopes, while American envelopes had the red and blue stripes identifying international mail.

The mailman would give the mail to Chief Master and leave. Chief Master looked at what he had received and every one of the ten or more instructors present in the do jang at the moment would stop their practice and sit around Chief Master, waiting for news. I would also sit and look at him when I saw there was mail from America, hoping Barry had written me a letter.

I was a Third Degree Black Belt at the time; I was the lowest-ranking instructor in the school at the moment. Clearly, I did not have the option of Chief Master reading Barry's letter to me in private. If I wanted to know what Barry had written in his letter, I had no choice but to sit and listen along with everyone else. I was so embarrassed when Chief Master read Barry's letters in front of everybody!

Chief Master would always open my letter first. All the instructors listened to what Barry had written, elbowing each other, giggling, and hooting. Both Barry and I knew this was going to happen, so neither of us wrote anything embarrassing. I have kept many of his letters with me. Here is one he wrote:

My Dear Choon-Ok:
I don't have time to write a long letter. Everybody here is fine. I hope to see you soon. Please, tell Chief Master Suh, your mother, and all family I said 'Hello.' Also please give my regards to all Kuk Sool masters.
I am writing for you with my heart open.
With love,
Barry

In his letters, he talked about general things and slowly we began to know each other. He said in another letter, "The weather is very beautiful today. The sun is shining and it's warm. When you come here I hope that we can go on many picnics. Do you like picnics? Tell me what you would like to do when you come here."

He also asked me to tell him about myself: "Tell me about yourself. Tell me things that you like and things you don't like!" And he told me about his hobbies: "My best hobby is motorcycle riding. I like riding motorcycles very much." He also asked me to send him things: "Please send me your ring size and also more pictures. Thank you."

With every letter he wrote and every reply I sent, we felt closer. But he did not say anything like, "I love you." Later, when I asked him why, he replied, "I couldn't say that. I hadn't met you yet." Barry had not met me, but he had a picture of me and he had seen my picture on the poster made for the demo in Hawaii. I, on the other hand, had no idea what he looked like at first. He sent me pictures later. I knew then how Mom must have felt when she did not even know what the man she was going to marry looked like.

Some of his words gave me hope about our future together: "Kuk Sool has made us together. I feel it is very good." We shared our passion for Kuk Sool. I felt it was a good thing to have that in common. The bond between us grew strong during the year we wrote to each other. "I believe that we will be together soon. I think about you 24 hours a day. Even though we are 11,000 miles apart, I feel very close to you." I began to feel the same way.

His letters made me feel that I would be welcome in his family. "My family very much wants to meet you. I gave them some pictures of you and they all think you are very beautiful. I hope you can meet my family soon. Also I wanted you to see my family. Enclosed are some pictures of my family at home in South Carolina during Christmas. I hope that you don't mind if I send you this pictures. My family would like to meet you. I know my family will like you, and I hope that you will like my family."

It made me happy that he remembered my birthday, February 16. He sent me a present: a beautiful music box I still have with me. When I replied, thanking him, he wrote, "I am very pleased that you liked your birthday present." I was also pleased that he wanted to meet my family. "I hope to meet your family soon," he wrote.

Sometimes we spoke on the phone, and it was a challenge to speak English, but I needed to practice. He was supportive of my efforts. "I

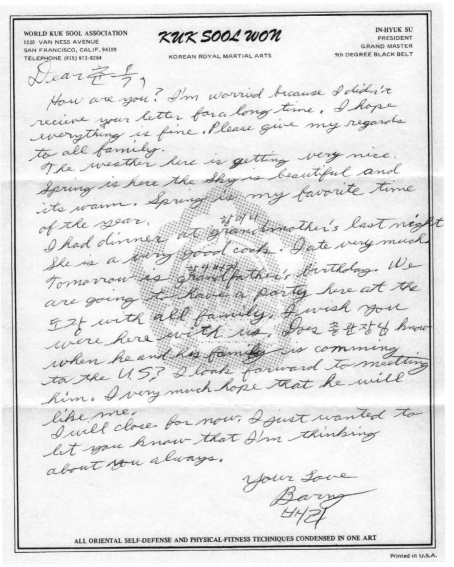

WORLD KUK SOOL ASSOCIATION
1030 VAN NESS AVENUE
SAN FRANCISCO, CALIF. 94109
TELEPHONE (415) 673-8264

KUK SOOL WON

KOREAN ROYAL MARTIAL ARTS

IN-HYUK SU
PRESIDENT
GRAND MASTER
9th DEGREE BLACK BELT

Dear 춘옥,

How are you? I'm worried because I didn't recieve your letter for a long time. I hope everything is fine. Please give my regards to all family.

The weather here is getting very nice. Spring is here the sky is beautiful and its warm. Spring is my favorite time of the year.

I had dinner at grandmother's last night. She is a very good cook. I ate very much. Tomorrow is grandfather's birthday. We are going to have a party here at the 도시 with all family. I wish you were here with us. Does 춘북장님 know when he and his family is comming to the U.S.? I look forward to meeting him. I very much hope that he will like me.

I will close for now. I just wanted to let you know that I'm thinking about you always.

Your Love
Barry
버리

ALL ORIENTAL SELF-DEFENSE AND PHYSICAL-FITNESS TECHNIQUES CONDENSED IN ONE ART

Printed in U.S.A.

Barry shows Choon-Ok he is practicing Korean.

very much liked talking to you on the telephone. Your English was very good!" He wanted me to know that we needed to close the language and cultural gaps between us; "Your brother [in-law] writes very good English. Also you must learn English well, and I promise to learn Korean well. I think you understand that because I am American and you are Korean we will have special problems, but if you understand and learn American

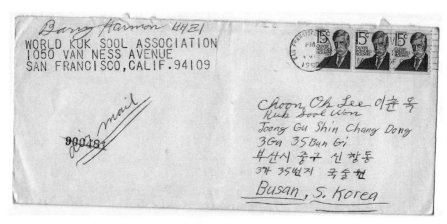

One of the envelopes Barry mailed, showing the date in the postmark.

customs and I understand and learn Korean customs we will be great and unbeatable together, because we will have the best of both worlds. This I speak truly from my heart. I believe we would be a good couple. Together we can win the world!" I believed that too.

Chapter 18

The Visa

After one year of exchanging letters, Barry came to Korea in late April of 1980. We were going to meet in person and he was going to introduce himself to my family. We were already making plans to get married later in 1980, as soon as I had a visa to travel to the United States. Barry had already applied for a "Fiancé Visa" for me from American immigration in 1979, and on my side I had started the paperwork to get my passport and other papers ready to immigrate to the United States.

We had decided that I would get a visa in Korea and travel with Barry to the United States where we would marry. If we got married in Korea first, then according to immigration regulations, I had to wait in Korea one year before I could move to the United States. Getting married in the United States was the best option, but sadly, that meant Mom would not be at my wedding. Kuk Sa Nim, Chief Master, and Choon-Up would be there, so my side of the family would be represented.

But things got complicated in March. Barry was very upset and wrote me a letter about the problem: "I am very angry now at the immigration department here in S.F. [San Francisco] I have been to the immigration department five times. Each time they tell me something different. My petition for a visa was approved Sept. 28, 1979. The immigration department here is supposed to send the information to the Seoul Embassy. I will go to the immigration department tomorrow and find out why they did not send the information to Korea. I am sorry that it is taking so long. Don't worry I will take care of everything here."

My visa had been approved, but the paperwork had not been sent to the American Embassy in Seoul yet. This might delay the process of stamping the visa in my passport and my move to the United States. We had submitted all the necessary papers. I even had an offer of employment by Kuk Sa Nim, which guaranteed I would not be a burden for the government.

When Barry traveled to Korea in late April to meet me and my family, we were not sure if the papers for my visa approval had already been sent to the American Embassy in Korea. We hoped they had been sent, but we were not sure. It was hard to confirm it at immigration in San Francisco. We were hoping I would get the visa stamped in my passport while Barry was in Korea, so we could travel together to America. I did not think much about this problem. I thought it would all work out as planned.

My dream was coming true, but with a bittersweet taste. I was moving to America with a good husband chosen by Kuk Sa Nim. I was going to continue my training side-by-side with my husband in a country where women are first and men second. But I was also leaving Mom, who had been my support all my life. My oldest brother would take care of her when she could not do it for herself, so I knew she was not completely on her own. I promised that I would try to visit Mom at least once a year.

I did not speak English well and I did not know American traditions. In many aspects, I did not know what to expect, but I was with family and would soon be married. My husband-to-be and I were going through the troubles of my visa together and getting to know each other through our

Choon-Ok spent as much time as possible with her mom between training sessions.

letters and telephone conversations. My life was about to change dramatically, but first I had to meet my husband-to-be in person.

Barry flew to Pusan to meet me and my family. I had pictures of him, so I had a good idea of what he looked like. One of the pictures showed a tall man dressed in a black Kuk Sool uniform with a black belt. I was very nervous about our first meeting. I wondered, almost like my mother when she was going to get married, what my future husband was really like. What color were his eyes? Would his eyes be one of the eye colors we didn't have in Korea? Were his eyes green? Gray? Maybe blue? I could not tell such details from the little photo he had sent me. I could only tell that he seemed to be tall. I wondered, but I was confident that Kuk Sa Nim had chosen the right husband for me.

The day Barry came to Korea, Choon-Up, Chief Master, and I went to pick him up at the airport. I was very nervous about meeting him. As it came time for him to arrive, my heart beat faster and faster. Up to then, all I knew about him and his character was what I had read in

Choon-Ok visited her mother often when she was not busy with training.

his letters, which did not reveal much of his real nature, because we knew the letters were not for our eyes only. My hands were sweating, and my heart was racing. I was going to meet my future husband, who would take me to a foreign country where the language and traditions were a mystery to me. I was waiting for him to step out of the airplane. Where was my big, tall American husband?

I was shocked when I saw him. I recognized his face instantly, but he was not like the big, tall man in the picture. His body was so small! In the picture he had sent me, he seemed to be very big and tall like most of the American men I had seen in

Barry Harmon when he was dating Choon-Ok.

movies and magazines. I thought all American men were big and tall, but the closer he came, the clearer I saw how he really was. His body was so small and so skinny! All I could see was his big nose!

He approached me and extended his hand. "How are you?" he asked, barely smiling. Barry faced Chief Master and Choon-Up and bowed deeply saying, "An young ha shim ni ka," which is the formal greeting in Korean. I thought he had very good manners, but he was so different from his picture.

While Barry was getting his luggage, Choon-Up whispered in my ear, "Wow, he is so small! I wish he were a little bigger." I just looked at her and smiled.

We took a taxi home to meet my mom and the rest of the family. My sister was having one of the best times of her life. She was really enjoying watching us meet for the first time, my look of surprise when I saw his real size and his big nose, our awkward formal hand shake, and our eyes trying to get all the details of each other's body and movement. We sat in the back seat of a tiny taxi. My sister got in first and sat by the window, I stepped in right after her, taking the middle seat, and Barry sat by my side. Chief Master sat in the front seat.

The taxi was so small that we were squished inside the back seat. Barry's arm was pressing tight against mine, shoulder to shoulder, and I could only stand it so long. I had to move his arm somehow, but I did not want to touch his arm. I grabbed his jacket, not his arm, by the sleeve with two fingers and threw it over my head to the back of the seat. Now that I think about it, it must have looked very silly and funny to my sister, who furtively looked at us and smiled to herself. Unfortunately, we were still squished. My shoulder was resting over Barry's heart now, and I could feel it beating fast. My heart was racing, too. My sister just looked at us and laughed.

We got home and found all my brothers and sisters and their families there, waiting with my mom to greet us and meet my future American husband. Barry and I bowed to my mom as soon as we stepped inside the door. Mom looked at him. She inspected his face and said to me that he had the face of a very nice man, the face of a gentleman, not the face of a mean man. She liked him right away.

"But he has a big nose," I told Mom. She smiled and went to the kitchen.

Barry did not speak Korean well yet. He did not know at the moment that Mom's first impression of him had been positive. He didn't know how she felt about him when they met, but he did not ask about it. He told me years later that he knew Mom liked him after we were married, but he was not certain about her feelings toward him when they met. This was the beginning of a long list of uncertainties and misunderstandings—some quite funny—we experienced because we did not speak each other's languages.

After Barry had been formally introduced to all my siblings, we got ready to have dinner together. I was cooking and Barry was sitting in the living room, speaking his best Korean and my brothers were speaking their best English, and he was watching me constantly. He could not keep his eyes off me. Around midnight, after dinner and after more conversation, we all went to our rooms to rest. Barry was staying at home with Mom and me while he was in Korea; he was going to sleep in my room and I slept in Mom's room.

Choon-Ok, Barry, Choon-Ok's mom, and her sister, Choon-Ja, during Barry's visit to Pusan.

Right before getting into my bed, I told Mom, "I want to say good night to my future husband."

"*No.* You cannot go into his room!" Mom said.

I laughed. "Don't worry," I said, "I just want to say good night."

Mom looked me in the eye and her lips formed a straight line. "Open my door and leave it open—the same with the door to his room. And do not step inside his room!" she commanded.

"Why?"

"Do as I just told you," Mom said. "Stand by the door, say good night, and come back here."

"OK," I replied. I opened his bedroom door, stuck my head inside, and quickly said, "Good night!"

Barry motioned for me to step inside the room, but Mom was watching me closely so I ran back to Mom's room. I heard Barry chuckling by himself inside the room.

Barry's first meeting with my family had been a positive one. He had made a good first impression and my family had liked him. However, they were still not completely sure about him being the best husband for me. He would be the first American, a foreigner to our culture and traditions, to be part of the family, so they had mixed feelings.

They did not know him at all. He had just arrived from the United States. Did he know, understand, and respect our traditions? Was he

Barry and Choon-Ok during Barry's visit to Pusan.

really a calm man as he appeared to be? When was he going to speak Korean well? Did he have any bad habits they didn't know about? My family had many questions that could hardly be answered in one meeting. But Barry had something big in his favor that meant a great deal to my family; Barry had been Kuk Sa Nim's choice for me, and this alone gave my family peace of mind about my future with him. He must have been a good choice, because Kuk Sa Nim had made the match for me. They trusted Kuk Sa Nim's judgment; nobody could make a better match for me than him. We all went to sleep soundly that night. Soon, I would be leaving for America and beginning a new life.

Chapter 19

"And You Want to Marry Her Because . . . ?"

We didn't give the visa application process too much thought. Barry had done all he could in San Francisco to process my visa, but the application did not run smoothly. Getting my visa to enter the United States seemed like it would be a simple formality. We would go to the American Embassy in Seoul and request my visa be stamped in my passport. We knew it had already been approved in September 1979. We hoped the paperwork for its approval had been sent to the Embassy. Then we would be ready to travel together to Los Angeles, California. I had been thinking more about what I would take with me. I was sad about leaving Mom, and I wondered what I would wear for the wedding. We hadn't even set a date for the wedding yet.

All this had to be placed on hold when the American Embassy denied my visa. We went to the Embassy in Seoul, hoping to get my visa, but instead they gave me a form indicating that my visa had not been issued because my application "did not comply with the provisions of" immigration. The Embassy said the visa was "pending report from INS/San Francisco." San Francisco Immigration had not sent the paperwork for my visa approval yet.

We were puzzled and upset that our marriage had to be postponed. We didn't want to marry in Korea and wait a year to reunite in the United States. Barry decided to request an appointment to speak with the consul in person and explain the situation. My visa had been approved in Washington, D.C.; the only problem was that San Francisco apparently had not sent the approval to the Embassy in Seoul yet.

I did not attend the meeting, but Barry told me all the details about it, as translated by Chief Master. After formal introductions, Barry presented our case to the consul and asked him the reasons for denying my visa. It had been approved in September 1979. He told the consul that we had been writing to each other for a year and that we

AMERICAN EMBASSY

Seoul, Korea

_4.29.80_
_____
Date

Sir: _LEE Choon Ok_

This office regrets to inform you that it is unable to issue
a visa to you because you have been found ineligible to receive
a visa under the following sections(s) of the Immigration and
Nationality Act, as amended: (Only the checked items apply to
your case.)

[ ]   Section 214(b) Which prohibits the issuance of a
                     temporary visitors visa to anyone who
                     fails to establish that he is a nonimmigrant
                     under the terms of the law.

[X]   Section 221(g) Which prohibits the issuance of a visa to
                     anyone whose application does not comply
                     with the provisions of the Immigration and
                     Nationality Act or regulations issued
                     pursuant thereto.

[ ]   Section

Further consideration will be given to your visa application
if you obtain and present to this office the following:

pending report from INS/San Francisco

                              Sincerely,

                              Patricia Hill Dick
                              American Vice Consul

FS-290A(NIV)
(6/15/79)

_Document from the American Embassy in Seoul, in which they inform Choon-Ok her
visa's approval is "pending report from INS (Immigration and Naturalization Service)/
San Francisco."_

were ready to formalize our relationship in marriage and begin our life together as a family in the United States. We both were honest, hard-working people who just wanted to get married and develop our careers in America. What could be wrong with that?

Barry felt frustrated during the meeting. The consul listened to him politely, but when it was time for him to plainly explain why the visa had been denied, the consul did not provide a straight, clear explanation. He digressed and did not make his point. He went on and on, talking about marriages arranged not for love, but for convenience. Though he did not tell Barry this directly, Barry understood what the consul was trying to tell him.

Immigration had found out that foreigners would marry American citizens, not with the honest intention of forming a family, but just to get legal immigration status for a foreign spouse to enter and live in the country. This was becoming a common practice. The consul specifically brought up the example of many recent cases of other martial arts teams. Members of the Korean team had paid American citizens to marry them. The couples would marry in the United States and live together for a few months, then get a divorce. The marriage was a farce—a temporary arrangement between a man and a woman so one of them could easily live legally in America, the land of opportunities. It was clear to Barry that, although the consul had not said it in so many words, he thought that we were getting married just so I could legally enter the United States. He did not believe that we really wanted to form a family; he thought ours was just another temporary marriage.

Barry was upset, but he stayed calm and told the consul that we had honest intentions to get married and stay that way. We were not going to get divorced in a few months; we wanted to develop our careers and have children. The consul nodded, but said that he had no proof that our intentions were as Barry said. To him, our case looked just like numerous others linked to martial arts teams. The consul stood up and shook Barry's hand. The interview was over.

When Barry returned to my home from the Embassy, I saw an aspect of his personality I had never seen before. I had never seen Barry upset, and at first I didn't know why he was angry. He spoke in quick English I did not understand; finally Chief Master translated for me. Barry was very frustrated that the consul had thought that we were lying and just trying to cheat American immigration. The consul had denied my visa and there was nothing we could do in Korea to change this.

Barry paced up and down in my home's living room, thinking out loud in English; I could not understand what he was planning. But I quickly realized that without a visa, my plan to get married had to be postponed. Would I ever be able to have a visa stamped in my passport? If not, then living in America, where women can make their dreams come true, would not be part of my future. Much was at stake for me—not just my marriage, but also my future as a Kuk Sool Won martial artist. What could we do?

I wanted to talk to Barry to calm him and reassure him, but the language barrier between us was just too great. I decided to simplify things and speak in broken Korean so that he could understand. I held his hand, looked into his eyes and told him, "Oo-ri harl-mu-ni; harl-ah-bu-ji kah-chi ka;" which was very broken Korean for, "We will travel to grandmother and grandfather ages together." I wanted us to grow old together as one.

Barry looked in my eyes and said, "Yes, we will."

Barry traveled back to the United States with Chief Master and his family. They were immigrating to the U.S. and Barry was going to help them, but I had to stay behind. I stayed in Korea with my mom and continued my training. Barry had a plan. The consul had said that he had no proof that our real intentions were to stay married, develop our careers, and form a family in America. Barry was going to convince him that these were our intentions exactly.

The day after he got back to the United States, Barry wrote me a wonderful letter reassuring me of his commitment, and said that he would do all that was necessary to get us together as soon as possible. "I've been back in the U.S. one day. I am very lonely without you. I miss you so much. I think about you all the time. Since we were together in Korea I love you more than ever. I think that together we will be happy the rest of our lives. I am so sad that we are not together. I will not rest until we are together. I will go to the immigration department tomorrow. I don't know what they will tell me to do but I will do whatever they say must be done."

He continued writing often, several times a month, and his letters now had a different tone. He was not distant and formal anymore; after all, we had met and spent time together during the two weeks he was in Korea with me and my family. But the problems obtaining my visa, the delay of our wedding, and the possibility that it might not happen at all brought us even closer. He kept me updated of his plans to get my visa every step of the way.

Barry spoke to all his family members, as well as friends who knew him well. He also spoke to members of the do jang in San Francisco, where Barry lived and trained with Kuk Sa Nim. He talked to as many people as he could think of and asked them to write letters to both the South Carolina Congressman and the California Congressman about us. He wanted his friends and family to tell the Congressmen that we were honestly planning to get married and stay that way, growing our careers and family. The testimonies our friends and family wrote to the Congressmen were to confirm and support our honest intentions to get married. The more people who supported us, the better the chance the Congressmen would write to the American Ambassador in Korea in our favor. Hopefully, all the letters from family, friends, and the Congressmen would convince the consul that we wanted to form a family, not just get legal status for me to live in America. Barry and I were happy and thankful that so many friends and family took the time to write their letters to help us.

Barry's sisters, brother, and his parents wrote letters, as did many of his friends. The letters not only supported our intentions, but respectfully asked the Congressmen to write to the American Consul in Korea, explaining that family and friends confirmed and supported our true intentions for marriage. Pastor Young Soon Park from the Korean Baptist Church, who was going to perform the ceremony of our marriage, also wrote a letter to the Congressmen, certifying our wedding plans and indicating the date scheduled for our wedding was May 25, 1980.

Barry's family was very supportive. His sister Robin wrote me a very nice letter. "I wanted to write you this letter to let you know that all of us—Mamma, Daddy, Carol, Hugh, Barry, myself and my husband, Clint, and Carol's husband, Russell—we are doing *everything* possible to get you to California so you and Barry can get married when you planned to. All of us are very excited about you and Barry getting married, and we are very anxious for you to come to South Carolina and be in our family. I know that you are upset and Barry is very upset but let your mind rest knowing that we are behind you and Barry, and we will see to it that everything works out. . . . Know that our family is yours, our thoughts are with you, and you and Barry are forever in our prayers."

I thank Robin for her strong support. I felt that I was part of the family already.

Family and friends of Barry vouched for his honesty and real intentions to marry a Korean woman who was willing to share his career and his life. We hoped that all these letters would be enough to convince the American Consul that we really wanted to get married. After the letters were mailed, we just had to wait.

Master K met me on my way out of the do jang. "I heard your American husband-to-be left without you to go back to America. Don't you think this is getting too complicated? How are you going to get a visa now?" he asked.

"We have a plan to convince the consul our intentions to marry are honest, sir," I said.

"You are a Korean woman, and a very pretty one. Look around you; I am a better husband for you. I am Korean like you," Master K said.

"I am not interested. I just want to be able to continue my training, sir," I said.

"What for? You are a good student, but there's only so much a woman can do in martial arts. This is for men, not for women. Training is tough and long. Women cannot do it. Only men can," he said.

"I have to go, sir." I hurried back home.

Two months after the letters our friends and family had written had been sent, the American Consulate in Seoul called me for an interview and asked me to bring my passport. I was very nervous the day of the interview. Would I get the visa stamped in my passport this time? I was also nervous because I did not speak English yet, and I had to go on my own.

I waited hours for my turn, but finally they called my name and I stepped inside a small office. The immigration officer already had my passport with him. He looked me up and down a couple of times, but he did not say a word. Silently, he flipped pages on my passport; when he found a clean page, he reached for a seal and stamped my passport with it. He looked at me again without speaking, closed the passport and wrote on the back "She cannot speak English." He handed the passport to me, stood up, and offered a hand shake. I shook his hand and left the small room, thrilled.

The letters and the long wait had paid off. I was going to marry Barry and live in America where women's dreams could come true. I felt very lucky that day and I could not wait for Barry to know about it. I had to plan my wedding now. Oh, no! What was I going to wear?

PART THREE

LIFE IN A NEW COUNTRY

Chapter 20

Going to America

It was my longest airplane trip ever, but this was the last thing on my mind. I was crossing the Pacific Ocean, all the way from Korea to North America. I had at least fifteen hours of flight to do nothing but think about my future. I was leaving Korea, my home for the first twenty-four years of my life and the only place, the only people, and the only language and lifestyle I had ever known.

I was leaving Mom. We had grown very close, because we had similar personalities and we had shared many life-changing experiences. She had saved me from the flood and always managed to feed us and clothe us, even during the hardest times. She was the only person I could count on. I was going to miss her very much.

But I was also leaving a tough life. I was going to change my future. I would not become a traditional Korean stay-at-home wife and mother, like my mom and sisters. This airplane ride was taking me to the United States, where I was going to meet my soon-to-be American husband who also practiced Kuk Sool Won. I trusted he was a good match for me because Kuk Sa Nim himself had selected him. I felt very hopeful that life was going to be good for me. I was going to continue practicing Kuk Sool Won with my husband and one day we would have our own place to live, our own school, and a family. My life was going to improve from now on. No more warmth-less, food-less, hopeless life. I was on my way to fulfilling my childhood dream, the dream of the little girl on the beach.

Many things were going to change for me, and I knew that it would not be easy to adapt. In a way, moving to America was similar to my move from Koje Do to Pusan, but moving to America was going to bring more changes. Now, not just the place was going to be different, but the people, language, traditions, customs, food, and even the weather were going to be new to me. And I knew so little about them.

For starters, I did not speak English. I knew just a few words like "thank you" and "please." That would be a challenge, but if others had learned English, I could too. Many other things would be different. Would I be able to eat Korean food often, or would I have to change and eat American food, which I did not like very much? What was the proper way to address my in-laws, especially my husband's parents? I knew I was going to be learning a new way of life as it presented itself to me, and taking a crash-course in American culture, so to speak. But it would all be worth it, because in return, I was going to have the opportunity to pursue my training for the rest of my life in a society where women's wishes were also considered in family decisions. I was not going back.

I arrived in Los Angeles, California in July of 1980. Barry and his best man Ken and his friend Charles were at the airport to pick me up. It was a sunny, cloudless day, and I thought that was a good sign of things to come. They were very happy to see me, and I was beaming too. Barry and I could not believe we were finally together after the long ordeal to get my visa. I was finally stepping on American soil!

Barry gave me a beautiful bouquet of flowers, a hug, and a kiss on the cheek. But the flowers were so wrong! I was surprised and a little angry when he gave me a bouquet of pink carnations. "What kind of welcome is this?" I thought. "These are the type of flowers you

Choon-Ok arrives in Los Angeles, California. Barry and his friend Ken welcome her with flowers.

give to your *mother* on Mother's Day, not your fiancé! He should have given me red roses; that's what you give to your fiancé. Well, that's what we do in Korea."

This was my first cultural clash and, although I was upset about the flowers for a while, I see now how it really didn't matter what type of flowers Barry gave me. Cultural differences were going to bring me many surprises. We flew to San Francisco, picked up Barry's car from the airport, and arrived in Kuk Sa Nim's home, where we would stay while preparing for the wedding, which would take place a couple of weeks later.

In San Francisco, I joined my sister, Chief Master, and their children again. It felt like when we lived in Korea together. Kuk Sa Nim's oldest sister was very kind to take care of the arrangements for my wedding, both the ceremony and the celebration, and I am very thankful for all she did. I did not have money to contribute, but I brought my wedding dress. I would be dressed neither in a Korean nor an American traditional wedding dress. I brought an elegant Korean long dress I had used in Kuk Sool celebrations. The dress was mostly white with fine embroidered details in pink. I added a long, white, delicate veil that dropped from my head to the floor and also covered my face. I held it on my head with a simple arrangement of flowers.

Everything seemed to be fine. But my sister was upset and Chief Master was upset. I could not understand why at first, but soon I realized they were disappointed and unhappy about my future.

"He does not have money!" Choon-Up said. "We thought he had it, and a place to live, but he doesn't."

"This is not what I had expected," said Chief Master. "I might as well send you back to Korea!"

"I am not leaving. I am staying, and I will marry him," I said.

My sister insisted. She asked me to go back and to find another husband. I said no a thousand times before my wedding day.

As Barry and I look back, we understand why Choon-Up and Chief Master did not want me to marry him. He had nothing. Not even money to go to the movies. If my daughters wanted to marry a man like him, I would definitely say no and so would my husband. I told them money didn't matter to me, but they continued to worry about my future and what would become of me.

We got married on July 13, 1980 in a small Presbyterian Church in Richmond, California, in the San Francisco Bay Area. There were guests from my side of the family, including Choon-Up, Chief Master, and their children, and Kuk Sa Nim and his family, including his mother and father, and other friends. On Barry's side, his mother, Adrianne Harmon, attended the ceremony as well as many of his friends. Barry's father, his sisters, brother, and their families could not attend. I was going to meet them at their home in South Carolina after the wedding.

Choon-Ok on her wedding day.

The day of my wedding, I was happy and sad at the same time. I was happy because I was marrying the man Kuk Sa Nim had picked as the best choice for me. This was the beginning of a new journey toward a future very different from the one I would have had if I had stayed in Korea and married a traditional Korean man. But I also had my family's discontent to deal with; they continued to insist that I not marry him, but return to Korea.

"Over my dead body!" Barry said when I told him about my family's wishes. We had decided to get married a long time ago and neither one of us would change our minds after all we had gone through to

Barry, Choon-Ok, friends, and family at their wedding.

Barry and Choon-Ok leaving the church after the wedding ceremony.

be together. Money or not, we were going to be together. It was hard to place all these thoughts aside and fully enjoy my wedding.

The ceremony was simple and beautiful. It was a bilingual ceremony, so both families would understand the language and feel included. Kuk Sa Nim's father held my hand and walked me down the aisle. As we walked down, step by step, I looked at Barry's face and it seemed as if he were smiling from his heart. I told myself, "This is my husband until I die." As I passed a friend, he repeated the old Korean saying that if the husband smiles when the bride walks down the aisle, the first child will be a daughter.

I heard them all say, "Barry, don't smile or your first child will be a daughter." That made me smile and think of my mom and wish she were here with me.

We listened to the priest, we exchanged vows, and at the end, the priest told Barry, "You may kiss the bride."

I was startled; I had never kissed anyone in public before and there was no way I was going to kiss him in front of all our family. Barry lifted my veil and leaned in to kiss me, but I quickly stuck both of my hands right in his chest and stopped him cold. I shook my head and said, "No, no, no" and everyone else said, "Yes, yes, yes!" Finally, I just let him kiss me on the cheek. He was so surprised I wouldn't kiss him, and I was so upset that everyone wanted me to kiss him in public. I was *not* going to kiss him in front of other people.

Our wedding celebration was very lively. We had many guests, abundant food and drinks, and a white wedding cake with three layers. My new husband was immediately immersed in a Korean wedding tradition, which is like a game or a joke played on the new couple. Two masters brought Barry to the center of the room, took his belt from his waist, and tied it around his ankles tight. A very large master grabbed Barry's feet, lifted him, and held him upside down with his hands. They had taken my husband "hostage" and it was up to me to set him free.

One of the masters looked at me and asked what I would give him so he would release my husband. Would I give him money? During all the "negotiations," Barry hung upside down and felt a little dizzy. Barry didn't know what to do except yell. He kept trying to talk them into letting him down and when that didn't work he tried to ask me for help.

Of course I did not have any money and I told them so. Very well then, the master continued, if I had no money to give for my husband's freedom, would I sing or dance in exchange for his release?

The wedding cake.

I was not enjoying this at all. I had nothing material to give for him, and I was not going to dance or sing. Not me.

"I don't care what you do with him," I said and sat down at the main table, ignoring them completely.

Barry begged me to do something. He was feeling quite dizzy by then, but I refused to sing or dance. He begged some more, and everybody laughed and clapped, but I did not dance or sing. Finally, they let him go for free. I was glad it was over.

Chapter 21

Honeymoon at the In-Laws'

The fourth airplane trip of my life was to South Carolina, to my in-laws' house by Lake Wateree where Barry and I spent our honeymoon . . . in the company of his family. I had only met Barry's mom, who attended the wedding, and now I met the rest of his immediate family. I met his dad, Robert Harmon, everybody called him Bob; his sisters, Robin and Carol, and their husbands; and his younger brother, Hugh.

I relaxed when we moved away from my family's pressure, but soon I realized that a different kind of tension was about to exist. To begin with, I was not going to hear a Korean word for a while—only English. And how should I behave? I had no clue about American social rules between me and my in-laws. Well, I decided I would do what I knew to do. I would do what I would have done if I had married a Korean man. I would show my utmost respect for Barry's father and obedience to his mother. I could not go wrong by showing respect.

They all came to the airport to welcome us and it was a very happy reception. As soon as they saw us coming down the aisle, they raised their arms and waved, calling Barry's name aloud, "Barry, Barry! Here we are!" They were smiling and very excited. I felt relieved that it was all very informal and I relaxed a bit.

I looked for Barry's father. I had to salute him first, very ceremoniously. He walked toward me and I walked toward him, both of us moving slowly and looking into each other's eyes. I stopped a few steps short of him and bowed deeply in front of him, with my arms by my side and looking down. After a few seconds, I straightened up and looked at him, but did not smile. He waited for me to finish my greeting, and then he took a couple of big steps in my direction and gave me a tight bear hug. He also said something I did not understand, but he was smiling and hugging me. I was terrified!

"You were as stiff as a board!" Barry told me later, laughing. Of course I was! I was so surprised. This would have never happened if I had a Korean father-in-law. I pushed him away and backed up, head down, waving my hands. "No, no!"

The rest of the family was also surprised, but took it lightly. They laughed in a friendly way and said incomprehensible words that sounded soothing. I relaxed a bit, but was at a complete loss about how to behave in the presence of Barry's parents.

At first, I did not talk much, just laughed often or smiled and nodded when they talked to me. I needed a crash course in English and Barry wanted to learn more Korean. We had an English-Korean and Korean-English pocket dictionary and used it to find the right words when gestures and charades did not get us through. I watched TV and it also helped me to learn more words. I began pointing at things and asking for their names in English. Some names were very funny, even musical to me, like a grocery store we visited called "Piggly Wiggly."

"We are going to the Piggly Wiggly."

"What is 'Wiggly Piggly'?" I asked. They pointed at the grocery store. I looked at the store's name above the door and tried to repeat "Piggly Wiggly" many times to get it right, but it always came out "Wiggly Piggly, Wiggly Piggly."

"Say 'Piggly Wiggly,' not 'Wiggly Piggy,'" they told me a few times.

I kept reversing the words like I reversed my hand movements when I was learning new techniques. We couldn't help it and laughed every time. I wondered, "What is 'Wiggly' anyway?" I did not learn its meaning until recently.

It was not just the language that was new to me; it was also the accent. South Carolina people did not sound like California people. I asked them constantly to repeat the names of things so I could get it right. My most common words were, "Ah? Say it again, please."

"What? 'Peggly Weggly?'"

"No, Piggly Wiggly."

"Wiggly Peggly?" What a tongue twister!

Barry's family was very patient and seemed to enjoy the process. They seemed to have a great deal of fun every time I said "Wiggly Piggly" and sometimes they asked me to repeat the name just because they thought the way I said it was cute. I had no idea why they all laughed so much every time I said it. I just thought it was hard to say and made no sense, but I went along with the joke.

I offered to teach them Korean words in exchange, but that proved harder for them than it was for me to learn English.

"How do you say 'Thank you' in Korean?"

"Kam sa hahm ni da."

"Kan *sa*mi da?"

"No, Kam sa hahm ni daaaa."

"Kan say mi daaaa?"

"No, Kam sa hahm ni *daaa*."

"Forget it! Thanks!"

I had better luck teaching one of Barry's young nieces. Rhiannon was three years old and she picked up Korean very quickly. She learned the correct pronunciation immediately and remembered the words. The first Korean word Rhiannon learned was "pae ko pa," which means "hungry." After that, she went around saying, "Aunt Choon-Ok, pae ko pa, pae ko pa." I loved it when she said it and rushed to fix her something to eat.

We spent two weeks in South Carolina and Barry's family made me feel like I belonged. We cooked together and I showed them a few Korean dishes which they enjoyed, especially kimchi. We laughed a lot, too.

I also had the opportunity to meet Barry's grandparents on his mother's side. Natives from the South Carolina countryside, they had never left it and had never seen an Asian person before. They had seen Asian people on TV or in the movies but never in person.

They were very kind, caring, and very curious about me. When we met, Barry and I bowed to both of them and they just looked at me. They didn't know what to do; they weren't sure if they should stand up or sit down. It seemed to be confusing to them, so I told Barry to tell them to sit on the couch to receive our bow.

After we finished bowing, Barry's grandparents approached me slowly and touched my arm with their fingers. Slowly and softly they slid their fingers up and down my arms and my long hair. I looked down; I was shy and did not know what to do. I just let them touch my arms and hair. Afterwards it seems that they couldn't take their eyes off me.

Grandmother prepared a very old-style, traditional Southern lunch. I remember ham, corn, and boiled vegetables, none of which I actually liked, because I was still used to Korean food. I do remember the one thing I liked—banana pudding. I had never had it before, but it was delicious. I liked it so much that I asked Barry's mom to teach me how to make it. She told me that it was a family recipe going back three generations and to pass it on to my children.

Barry's grandparents told him that I was very pretty.

His grandfather looked at him and said, "You are very lucky to have found her. Boy, with a woman like this, you just have to give her flowers sometimes."

Barry was happy I had made a good impression on his grandparents. I hoped he remembered roses were the right flowers next time.

My English was improving, but conversations with my in-laws were mostly by gestures, checking out the dictionary, pointing at objects, and repeating new words. Cultural differences made good stock for embarrassment and humor at the same time.

One morning, Barry, his mother and father, and I went to the grocery store— "Piggly Wiggly," of course. Barry and his mother entered the store, picked up a cart, and headed for an aisle. After a few minutes, Barry noticed that his father and I were not around. They wondered where we were and Barry began looking for us. He searched nearby aisles, but he did not see us. Finally, he returned to the main entrance and there we were.

Barry's dad and I had both stopped in front of the main door. I was bowing at him and waiting for him to enter, because he had seniority and respect mandated that he enter the store first. I would follow him. But his rules were different than mine. As an American gentleman, he was courteous and let ladies go first. He extended his arm, palm up toward the door, indicating me to enter first. That was not the right thing to do from my perspective. In Korea, seniors always go first. I bowed to him and waited for him to cross the entrance. He shook his head and pointed at the door one more time. I bowed and waited. He pointed at the door. We were caught up in this bowing and pointing routine. Neither one of us wanted to be disrespectful to the other one. Then Barry found us.

He couldn't figure out what we were doing at first, but when he realized that we were caught up on a cultural crossroads, he laughed. He tried to talk me into going first, but I shook my head and bowed at his father. Barry's dad insisted ladies go first. Because neither one of us would give up our tradition, Barry took action, grabbed my hand, and pulled me inside the grocery store. I had to follow my husband, so I went in first, but felt very unhappy. "We have to finish shopping *today*," Barry told me, smiling.

Chapter 22

"He Has No Money!"

Our two-week-long honeymoon with my in-laws went by fast. Soon, it was time to go back to California to resume our training. I was looking forward to finding our own place to stay—a place we could call home. I was dreaming of sleeping on an American-Style bed and other simple comforts I had seen in magazines and movies. As it turned out, I would have to wait for my dream to come true. Especially sleeping in an American-style bed. We did not have money and Barry did not have a job. For the last five years, Barry's job had been to eat, sleep, and train under the watchful eye of Kuk Sa Nim, which included teaching classes at the headquarters. But Barry did not have any money because his training was in the traditional style of living with the teacher, who took care of all his needs, just as I had lived with Chief Master and my sister while I was training in Korea.

We arrived in San José, California and moved in with Chief Master, Choon-Up, and their children. Master K had come to America with Chief Master and he was living there too. He also wanted to have his own school in America. My sister and Chief Master were still unhappy about my financial situation.

"You should go back to Korea," they repeated. "He has no money and no job." I had refused to go back before I got married, and I certainly was not going to now that I was married. "I am staying here and I am staying married," I replied.

For the next six or eight months, Barry helped Chief Master and his family to get established in San José. They were still learning English, they did not drive, and they were not familiar with the area. Barry helped them by taking them to all the places they needed to go, opening and managing bank accounts, and helping with any other issues they needed assistance with. I helped my sister like I had in Pusan. I babysat her children and helped with house chores.

Barry and I also dedicated time to continuing our training with Kuk Sa Nim; there was no time for Barry to work. We focused on our training and on helping our masters. One day, we would open our own school and teach Kuk Sool Won to our own students. We wanted to achieve master level, which is Fifth Degree Black Belt, and then continue to reach the highest ranks. Soon we learned that not everybody supported our goals.

Chief Master was going to open his own school, but the property needed remodeling before he could welcome his new students. Barry and other students, including Master K, helped fix the building. There were walls to paint, shelves to hang on the walls, floors to clean, and furniture to move in. Barry helped with all of these, but the situation became very tense. I was not there, but he told me about it later when we were alone.

"So you think you will be the first American Kuk Sool Won master?" asked Master K.

"I am training for my Fifth Degree testing, sir," said Barry.

"And Choon-Ok thinks she will be the first woman master in Kuk Sool Won?"

"Choon-Ok is training too, sir. We train together every day," Barry said.

"You two together, ha? How nice. She trained with me in Korea, you know?" said Master K.

"Yes, sir," said Barry. He was nailing bookshelves to a wall.

"You have very ambitious goals, you know. Too ambitious for both of you," said Master K.

"We have decided to dedicate our lives to Kuk Sool Won, sir," said Barry, aiming at a nail.

"What do you think you are doing with that hammer? Give it to me; I'll show you how it's done!" said Master K. "How can you be a master when you cannot even hit a nail right?"

I think Master K was very jealous, because he had invited me to the movies and dinner many times in Korea and I had not accepted his invitations. He had a hard time accepting that I had married someone else, especially a Westerner.

I helped my sister with her children and house chores, and I trained every day with Barry. Barry helped our masters get established and with Chief Master's remodeling. That was all we could do for the moment. We ignored the pressure and focused on our training; we wanted to be ready for the test of Fifth Degree Black Belt, the master level.

Choon-Ok and Barry focused on training.

"I still think you should go back to Korea," said Choon-Up again while we were cooking dinner one night. "How can you live in this country with a husband who has no job and no money?"

"I am staying married and staying here," I said. "We'll do fine. I've lived worse before, and we'll do better in the future when we have our own school."

"I am thinking of what's best for you," said Choon-Up.

"I know, but I'll be OK. Don't worry," I said.

In 1981, our masters did not need Barry's help as much. Now he had more time on his hands; he found a job. He worked first as the assistant manager of a Taco Bell restaurant; he also worked on a windshield repair business. These were not exactly his favorite jobs, but they helped us save money to start our own school. I had also found a job working in a factory soldering computer boards. I worked from 7:30 a.m. to 3:00 p.m while Barry worked from 4:00 p.m. to 1:00 a.m. He would drop me off and pick me up in the afternoon, then go to work. We did not see much of each other for those eight months that we both worked at those jobs. I was glad when we could quit those jobs and have our own school.

After eight months working, we found a good place for a school in San Mateo, California. We had saved part of the money needed to rent and fix the place and Chief Master lent us the rest—enough to start and cover the first month's rent. The place needed remodeling too, and we worked on it when we were not training. We did not have extra money to rent an apartment, so we lived in our school.

We had separate dressing rooms for men and women and we slept, cooked, and washed our clothes and dishes in the lady's dressing room. We cooked on a small electric hot plate and washed the dishes in the bathroom sink. We slept in our Korean-style bed.

Every night, I unrolled the thick comforter, like a thin mattress, and we covered ourselves with a sheet and a blanket. Every morning, I rolled our bed back up and tucked it away. Oh, how I would have liked to have had an American-style bed! I knew it wouldn't fit in the dressing room; I could only dream of the day I would have one. I picked up our dishes and cups and our hot plate and stored them in a cabinet so our students could use the dressing room. This was our home for quite a while. We were improving; we had started our own school and had our own place to live. We were together and doing what we wanted to do—continuing our training. We were hopeful things would get better in time.

Our life was very busy for the next six years between our training and taking care of our school. Our training also involved public demonstrations at schools and participation in tournaments around the country. We traveled to Korea once a year for more training, and I had the opportunity to visit my mom and the rest of my family on these trips.

When we traveled to Korea, we usually went as a group with other Kuk Sool masters and students of many different ranks. During those wonderful times, we not only trained but also traveled around the country by bus and many times the long drives became a little boring. One time, during a trip in 2002, I decided to lift the boredom by asking the people on the bus to sing karaoke style. Unfortunately, they agreed only if I would lead the way. I did not know many songs in English, but I knew the children's song "The Itsy Bitsy Spider," and so did most of the people on the bus, so that's what we sang.

I began singing and the others joined me in good spirits. I thought we were doing very well and that everybody was cheering up when I heard them laughing every time I said, "The itsy bitsy spider." They were laughing very hard. I did not understand what was so funny that they could not stop laughing.

I stopped singing and asked them, "Why are you laughing so hard?" They did not want to tell me why, but I insisted.

Finally, one of them explained to me that when I sang, "The itsy bitsy spider," it actually came out the "The itchy bitchy spider" thanks to my mispronunciations in my Korean accent.

After they explained to me the difference between an "itsy bitsy spider" and an "itchy bitchy spider" I finally understood what was so funny about my song. That *was* funny! I laughed with them and that became one of the famous jokes of our trips to Korea. Those were the kind of good times that helped me overcome tough times.

Barry wrote a newsletter for Kuk Sa Nim's school. It provided school news to the students, introduced the school masters, and informed students about activities, special programs, and important dates like testing and belt promotions.

One day, Master K called Barry for a private meeting. He did not say what it was about. When Barry entered the room, he found that four other Kuk Sool masters were present and sitting, forming a circle. Neither Kuk Sa Nim nor Chief Master were present. Master K told Barry to sit in the middle of the circle. Master K placed a copy of the latest newsletter in front of him. He pointed to a list of names on the margin of the first page of the newsletter and said:

"Why did you list Chief Master's name like this?"

"What's wrong with it, sir?" asked Barry, trying to see the list.

"This is a very disrespectful way to write Chief Master's name!" said Master K. The other masters nodded and murmured.

"I apologize, sir, but I don't understand what you mean. Let me see the newsletter," said Barry.

"How can you aspire to be a Kuk Sool master, the first American master, when you cannot even write in English!" said Master K. The other masters nodded and whispered something.

"I did not intend to offend anybody, sir. It has to be a mistake," said Barry.

"This is the utmost disrespect. No Kuk Sool master would do a thing like this," said Master K, looking at the other masters. They nodded and looked at Barry.

"I am sure this is a mistake, sir. I will fix it, but I have to go now," said Barry. He got up and left the room quickly.

I was waiting for him to come back to the do jang and tell me what had happened during the meeting, but hours passed and he did not return. I began to worry. I knew he was concerned when he left for the meeting, because Master K and the other masters opposed his intentions of becoming a master. He wondered what would be discussed in this last-minute meeting. I decided that the best I could do was to wait for him to come home. But I was worried. When he returned home, it was very late. He said that he needed to leave in order to calm down. I asked him to never leave again without telling me. I was so worried! He agreed and apologized for leaving me so abruptly. I was thankful for the good relationship I had with my husband, especially when my family continued feeling unhappy about the way we lived.

"I don't know how you can stand living in that tiny room. It is not even a bedroom; it's a dressing room!" said Choon-Up.

"I've lived in worse places before. I am fine. We are together, we are training, we have our school, and I am happy. Don't you worry," I said.

"Your life would be better in Korea. It would not be worse than what you have here," my sister said.

"I am staying here; I am staying married. I am doing what I want to do and things will get better as our school grows," I said.

"I just want what's best for you," Choon-Up said.

"I am fine, sister. Don't you worry."

Chapter 23

Accidents

Training got tougher as we learned advanced techniques and forms, and I had to focus even harder and longer. I practiced over and over for hours, repeating the movements until I got them right and did not have to think about what to do step-by-step. I practiced until one movement followed the next, naturally and smoothly, like second nature. I practiced daily with Barry and on my own.

We learned long sequences of movements or forms using long swords and short swords, and this required intense concentration because the weapons were sharp. One of those long forms was "Gum Dae Ryun," in which a man uses one long sword and a woman uses two short swords to perform a series of defense and attack movements. Barry and I had been practicing this form for quite some time now and had reached the point of doing it very quickly. It was coming along very smoothly, and we were ready to demo during a tournament.

One night, during one more practice of "Gum Dae Ryun," I came a bit short in one of my defensive movements. We had almost finished the sword form, and Barry had taken away one of my short swords and was attacking me with it. Raising the short sword with his right hand, he moved to stab me and I raised my right arm above my head to block his arm and prevent the strike when we heard a clang: the sword had stabbed my head. I had not raised my hand high enough to block the strike effectively and the tip of the short sword hit hard on my scalp. We stopped. I felt nothing right away, but then what felt like warm, thick tears began streaming down my forehead. It was blood coming down from the cut in my scalp.

"Oh, no! I killed my wife!" Barry cried. His face was pallid and strained when he saw three of four small streams of blood trickling down my face. I felt the pain, but did not pass out.

Barry cleaned my face and checked the wound and saw it was superficial. He applied pressure on my scalp with a cloth to stop the bleeding. It took a while, but finally the blood stopped flowing. Fortunately, I did not need stitches. I took pain medicine and did not think more about it. Some people asked me later if I would do the same form again. What if I was stabbed again, this time deeper? "I don't think about that," I told them. I was not going to let a small accident stop me from training. Accidents happen and they are like tough teachers. They teach you where you are making mistakes. This one taught me I had to make sure I raised my arm higher to block that attack if I did not want the sharp tip of the short sword to strike my scalp again.

Practicing for another demo became another tough teacher, this time teaching me about precision and control of my punches. On this occasion, I was practicing pushing an apple through a sword using my punches. Barry was holding a long sword horizontally with both hands, supporting the sword against his abdomen. Hanging from the tip of the long sword was an apple. I was to punch the apple with controlled strikes, making it slide a few times along the sword. I had to control my punches. I had to punch the apple strongly enough to make it move without touching the sharp sword.

I had practiced this many times successfully. I had determined the best distance between me and the sword so my punches reached the apple when my arm was fully extended as I punched. I had found the right, controlled force with which to punch just the apple, and not hit the sharp point of the sword. I felt I was ready for the demo.

Three weeks before the demo, I was practicing punching the apple when the accident happened. I punched as I had hundreds of times, but this time hit more than just the apple. The tip of the sword slid between two knuckles. Barry told me he knew immediately something had gone wrong when he felt the handle of the sword, which was resting on his abdomen, thrust into his body. That was not supposed to happen. My punches had to be so controlled that only the apple received the impact, not the sword.

I slid my hand out of the sword and it began to bleed profusely. We rushed to the emergency room, where they cleaned and inspected the wound. I was in a great deal of pain, but I kept a straight face. I knew the pain was temporary. It would go away soon after they gave me medication for it. I was very lucky this time. I had not sliced anything inside my hand but flesh. I could move all my fingers without a problem, but they stitched the wound because it was about an inch deep. I still have the scar to this day.

The doctors and nurses at the emergency room were puzzled. "How did this happen?" they asked. They had not seen a wound like this before. We thought about it and decided not to tell them I had been punching an apple on a sword. What would they think about that? We told them that a knife had fallen into the kitchen sink's drain and I had stuck my hand inside, looking for it, accidentally stabbing myself. What worried me the most was that I had a demo in three weeks. Would my hand be ready then?

People asked me, "Are you still doing the demo? What if you cut yourself again?" I was apprehensive of course, but I had to do it. Part of our training and way of life is that we overcome our fears; we do not let them limit or control what we can do. We learn what we did wrong the first time and make the necessary corrections. We face our fears and strive to overcome them. Furthermore, Kuk Sa Nim was expecting me to do it as planned. I could not disappoint him; I had to do it. This injury was not so severe that I could not complete the technique again. A few days before the demo, the doctor removed the stitches. My hand was sore, but I could move it normally. I practiced more. I focused intently, learning from the accident, and performed in front of a large crowd. This time, the apple slid a short distance every time I punched it and I did not touch the tip of the sword.

Chapter 24

"What Are You Doing With My Sword?"

Barry enrolled in the San Francisco College of Acupuncture & Oriental Medicine to study acupuncture. He also attended San Francisco State University and studied psychosomatics and alternative healing there. Our Masters had studied acupuncture and alternative healing and Barry wanted to follow in their steps and learn these methods, too. I took care of our school and taught on my own during the mornings and early afternoons while he was in class. When he returned home, he helped with the evening classes.

We had slowly added training equipment to our school, such as mats, targets for kicking and punching, wooden practice swords, metal swords, long and short staffs, and rubber knives. Sometimes we borrowed equipment from other schools, sometimes we brought it with us from Korea during one of our trips, or purchased it in the United States. Everything was very valuable to us, because it was expensive to have.

I was alone in the school; classes had not started yet, but the doors were open. I went to the restroom and when I returned to the front of the school, I saw that a man had walked onto the practice floor and taken one of the metal swords hanging on the wall. He held it with two hands and inspected it with great curiosity. He walked with it toward the door. I could not believe he was walking away with one of my precious swords. He was also wearing shoes in the practice area. Stepping onto the practice floor with shoes on is very disrespectful to other students. This man was being disrespectful and trying to steal!

"Where are you going with my sword?" I demanded, raising my voice and following him.

He stopped and turned to look at me. "I just want to look at it," he said. There was no expression on his face. I walked toward him and took the sword from his hands.

"Now, go away!" I did not want to talk to him; I wanted him to leave.

Choon-Ok in her do jang in front of the school weapons. Notice the sign: "DO NOT TOUCH WEAPONS."

He said something to me but I could not understand a word; however, I could definitely understand the gestures he was making.

He stood straight in front of me and placed his hands on his hips. In Korea, this is a challenging posture. He laughed at me, daring me to do something to stop him. He laughed in my face after he had taken *my* sword! I was furious. I was so angry that all I wanted to do was go after him.

With a quick, swift movement, I unsheathed the sword with my right hand, dropped the sheath, and held the sword with two hands over my head. "Get out!" I demanded. "Out of my school!"

His smile faded and his eyes opened wide; he was terrified. He realized he had seriously underestimated me and that I was coming after him with a sword. He backed up slowly towards the door without taking his eyes off me. When he reached the door, he turned quickly and ran down the street. I chased him with the sword held up over my head. I stopped just outside of my school as he crossed the street, stopped running, and watched me. It was a lonely street in the middle of a sunny California morning. There were no cars driving by or people close to us. "Come back here!" I demanded. He shook his head, his eyes wide.

I had scared him away; just what I wanted. I did not chase him any longer. He turned his back to me and ran fast down El Camino Street. I never saw him again. Thinking back, I am glad he ran, because I was extremely angry and might have cut him with my sword. This would have caused me immeasurable legal problems, and my martial arts career and my childhood dreams would have ended right there. Mom was right again; I had to watch my temper, because it could get me into serious trouble. I always felt I had to prove myself to others, in both Korea and the United States. Just like the man who tried to take the sword from my school, many people do not believe I am a true martial artist. They look at me and think I am bluffing and that they can easily put me in my place. They soon realize that I can support my claims.

One of our strategies to promote our school and attract new students was to distribute fliers to high school students as they were coming out of school. I went to high schools and stood by the nearby public bus stop, giving fliers to students and other people as they were getting on and off the bus. One day, I gave the flier to a group of three high school boys. They were tall, above six foot, and built big. I would say they were football players. When I gave the flier to one of them, he laughed and said, "Are you a black belt?"

"Yes, I am the instructor," I said, keeping a straight face. He looked at the other boys, laughing, and they imitated him. The young man that had spoken had an empty glass bottle in his hands, a soft drink I think. He grabbed the bottle by the neck and broke the bottom against the edge of the sidewalk.

"OK, I am going to attack you with the bottle. What are *you* going to do? Would you try to do something or would you run away?" he said.

Here was a young American man acting much like many Korean young men who did not believe I was a martial artist. I felt angry, but this time I controlled my temper and used my head.

"Sure, I'll fight you," I said, lowering my voice and looking him in the eye. "But if I do, I can really hurt you or even kill you. So, do *you* want to fight?" He stopped laughing and I continued talking. "I can fight, but you are a huge guy and I am a little woman. If I fight you, I may need to do something really hard on you to defend myself. If I make a mistake, I might kill you. You would be lucky if you didn't die."

He looked at his friends, as if he was asking, "Is she bluffing or is she for real?"

I asked one of the other young men, "Open your notebook and

write this on a piece of paper: 'In case I make a mistake and he dies, it's not my responsibility. It's his responsibility, because he's asking me to fight him.' If you write that down and you sign it," I said, looking at the guy with the broken glass bottle, "then I will fight you right now." I put down my fliers and told him again, "I will fight you right now!"

The young man with the broken glass bottle backed up. "Come here, do not back up. Just sign the paper and I'll show you what I can do. I won't fight you if you don't sign the paper, because I don't want to go to jail. I have a school and I have students to teach. It's you who is challenging me to fight. Sign the paper and we can do it right now." They turned around and left. They rushed down the street, looking back from time to time to see if I was following them. "Come visit my school," I told them loudly so they could hear me.

I shook my head in disbelief. People could challenge me even in the most peaceful situations. I had not been worried at all by this confrontation. I was happy I had controlled my first impulse to fight. I also told myself, "This is nothing. Since I was born and throughout my life, there have been so many times I could have died. I could have died of hunger, cold, accidents, or from physical attacks. This was nothing! This was not my time to die."

On the other hand, Barry was very concerned when I told him about the little incident. He told me not to distribute fliers alone anymore. "I don't want to lose my wife," he said.

I even had to convince my own students that I was a true martial artist! Fritz H. is a big man—six-foot, five-inches tall and about 230 pounds. He was a beginner student, a white belt, in our San Mateo school. Many years later, he told me that I had convinced him that Kuk Sool was the right martial art for him. I was curious, how that had happened.

I had a class at lunch time and he showed up at the school while I was teaching techniques in this class. He wanted to see what was going on in advanced classes. He also wanted to see how I taught. He had heard that I was a serious instructor, and he wanted to experience that.

I was about to teach a new technique to my students—Ki Bohn Soo number eleven—and decided to ask Fritz to be my partner and help me demonstrate the technique to the students. This technique was new to Fritz, and he told me that he was surprised when I asked him to be my partner. He told me that he thought that, because he was quite a bit larger than me, this would be interesting. He took his shoes off and walked onto the practice floor. I'll let him describe what he experienced in his own words:

"As Master Harmon began and struck the pressure points on my wrists, I changed my mind about her abilities, because it hurt. When she pressed on a pressure point on my neck, I wanted to scream, especially when she pushed up under my jaw. The next thing I knew, Master Harmon spun me around and I was on the ground with her knee on my neck, her hand on the other side of my carotid artery, and I was just about to pass out."

I finished the demonstration of the technique and released my grip. Fritz was fine, maybe a little sore, but no real harm was done.

"Afterwards, I was standing there, reviewing the whole thing and I remember saying to myself that if this petite woman could do that to me so casually, just to demonstrate this technique, I had arrived at a martial art that I could practice for the rest of my life. I can still feel what it all felt like right now, twenty years later," he said of the experience.

Fritz is now a Kuk Sool master, Kwang Jang Nim Fritz, and has his own Kuk Sool school in Tennessee.

Training, teaching students, and managing our school occupied all our time. As the date for testing for master or Fifth Degree Black Belt approached, we felt nervous and excited. If all went well, we would reach the master level, one of our major goals in life. But it was a goal that did not please others.

Master K had prejudiced many masters against us. On various occasions, we overheard him talking about our plans. "Kuk Sool should be for Koreans only," we heard Master K say to a group of masters. "How can he aspire to be promoted to Fifth Degree? It's true he is a diligent, good student, but he is an American, not Korean. And a woman master? A woman cannot achieve a man's level in martial arts. They are weaker. She would not last the master's test."

The constant lobbying against us felt like an uphill battle. At the master-level test, a panel of judges would decide if we qualified as masters. Many of the people Master K spoke to would be on that panel, deciding our fate. But we let it all pass. We had to test in front of all the masters regardless of how we felt. What mattered was that we focused on our training, both physically and mentally.

Chapter 25

Testing for Master Level

Testing was held in March 1985. Barry and I joined other students who were testing for other black belt degrees. We were the only ones testing for Fifth Degree.

Testing took place at headquarters, which was the school headed by Kuk Sa Nim. The students gathered on the practice floor. We spread the mats, and I made sure my two partners in testing were present. They were black belt students who would assist me in demonstrating self-defense and throwing techniques. I had two partners, because there were so many techniques to test for master level that it would be too much for one person to take all the falling during the test.

I was going to take the test in front of Kuk Sa Nim, Chief Master, and three other high-level masters sitting at a table. They had my testing form in front of them and they would record my performance as the test progressed. On each corner of the square practice floor sat one more judging master. Master K was one of the corner judges scoring me. Barry was going to test after me with the same judges presiding. The masters at the table would take turns asking me for techniques and forms to perform. Whatever they asked me to do, it was my responsibility to try my best to do it.

They would also evaluate my etiquette during the test, which is a very important part of Kuk Sool. Would I bow to my partner before we performed each and every technique? Would I bow again at the end? Would I treat my partner with respect and thank him for his assistance with a proper handshake at the end of the test? Would I respond to the masters' questions ending with "sir"? The masters would set the pace of the test; they could ask me to show them anything I had learned in Kuk Sool since I had started when I was fourteen years old. I was now twenty-eight years old.

The test began. First the masters asked me to demonstrate beginner's

Choon-Ok during her Fifth Degree Black Belt test.

techniques. I was expected not only to know them perfectly, but to perform them smoothly, demonstrating my persistent practice. One of my partners and I stood in front of each other in attention position: feet together, hands on belt, and eyes forward. Not a sound disturbed the practice floor. One master called a technique and I answered "Yes, sir!" I bowed, I kept low stances, I performed the technique, and I yelled a martial arts' yell—ki op—to release my energy. I bowed. Next technique: "Yes, sir!" I bowed, I kept low stances, I performed the technique, I ki op'd, and bowed to my partner. I continued with the next technique, and the next, and the next.

We moved on to the intermediate-level techniques without a break for resting or water. They called techniques at random, and I was expected to demonstrate them right away, without hesitation or mistakes. Every time a master called a technique I answered, "Yes, sir!" I bowed, I kept low stances, I did the technique, I ki op'd, and I bowed.

On one occasion, I was performing a self-defense technique in which I had to strike my partner with my palm, and I hit him too hard. He had to sit on the side to catch his breath. He was fine, but he could

Choon-Ok exhibits her skills and technique during her Fifth Degree Black Belt test.

not continue helping me right away. My other partner replaced him immediately to continue the test. The advanced-level techniques were next, then I moved to show my forms, and then I showed my skills with weapons, sword, long and short staff, and knife. For two continuous hours, I performed without stopping in front of the masters. They offered me breaks to rest and get water, but I said no. I was not going to show any signs of weakness.

During the whole test the only things you could hear were the voices of the masters calling the technique or form, "Yes, sir!," ki op, and the thud of my partner falling on the mat. Other students gathered around to observe, but nobody talked. A friend told me later that he had never seen such a strenuous and demanding test. When all the material had been covered to the satisfaction of the masters at the table, they declared the test finished. I had finished; I had shown all that I had learned. It was a real test of physical and mental endurance. All my training and daily practice had paid off.

Because I was the first woman to take the master level test, and

Barry was the first non-Korean man to take the test, our tests were more demanding than the average master test. Because of these special circumstances, more judges were present and more material was covered in our test. Our tests were setting a precedent for future master level tests.

Barry tested after I did, following a routine similar to mine. He also had two partners and the same judges and performed for them for almost two hours without stopping. Physical and mental endurance, smoothness, memory, etiquette, and everything else was tested and evaluated by the masters at the table and the four corner judges. We would have to wait a few days to know the results—to know if we had passed—to know if we had earned the title of Kuk Sool Won masters. We were exhausted, but happy that we had finished testing. Now it was all in the hands of the judges.

We were not there, so we don't know what happened exactly. Reliable sources told us later that our testing had created a very tense situation among the masters. All the masters at the test table and the corner judges, including Kuk Sa Nim, Chief Master, and Master K, met behind closed doors and discussed our performance to decide if we deserved to receive the title of master. It seems that no one had any objections about our performance; their only objections were about who we were—an American and a woman.

We know there were votes against us receiving the Fifth Degree. We know there were votes in favor. We know there were heated arguments against giving the title of master to a non-Korean man. We know there were also heated arguments against giving the title of Fifth Degree to a woman. Nobody had heard of such things before. We know that for a long time the arguments persisted, and patience grew thin. We know Kuk Sa Nim finally said, "If these arguments persist any longer, I will promote them, not to Fifth Degree, but to Sixth Degree right now!" which was one degree above some of the masters present. We know he could have done it; he was the Grand Master, and nobody was above him in Kuk Sool Won. We know this ended the discussion.

We received our promotion to the Fifth Degree Black Belt or master level in a ceremony at headquarters in 1985. We exchanged our black belt for a white belt. The four-inch-thick white belt is ceremonial and symbolizes a new beginning. We had reached the level of master; we were now ready to begin learning toward an even higher level. We would always be students, we would always need to practice more, and

Choon-Ok and Barry receive the degree of masters and wear the white belt of a beginner again during the ceremony.

there would always be room for improvement. After the promotion ceremony, we continued our training and continued teaching students in our school. We wore black belts when training and teaching, and did not wear the ceremonial belt then. Our titles changed when we achieved mastery. I now called my husband Barry Kwang Jang Nim most of the time, especially if we were around other people. This is the proper way to address a Kuk Sool master who has achieved Fifth Degree Black Belt or above. In a similar way, since I achieved my Fifth Degree Black Belt, my title has been Yuh Kwang Jang Nim. The word "Yuh" at the beginning of the title means 'female.' At home it's different. I call my husband "yuh-boh," which means "honey," and he calls me "yuh-boh" too. I thought that it was a good time to start a family.

Chapter 26

Becoming Parents

My maternal clock was ticking. I would soon be thirty years old, and I did not want to wait much longer to have children. Barry accepted that we should start trying to have a baby, but I was not sure of his feelings toward kids.

In the school, he did not like to teach the youngest students; he always asked me to teach them. Some kids did not follow directions right away; they played around and did not pay attention. It was more rewarding to him to teach adults or older teens, because they were more disciplined and focused on the training. Was this a sign that he did not like children? What would be his reaction to our baby if we had one? Would he be like my dad, who did not even want to look at me when I was born? That fear did not leave me alone. What would I do if he did not like our baby? Well, I could leave. Or I could make him leave . . . I had to wait and see.

I continued to practice carefully and to teach all through my pregnancy. By the end of the pregnancy, my stomach was so big that I could only kick to knee height. One night, at the end of class—it was about ten o'clock—we were leaving to go home. I climbed in our van and my water broke. Barry took me straight to the hospital. The doctor took one look at me and said, "The baby is coming tonight." She checked me into the hospital and prepared what was necessary for the delivery.

The contractions started, but by three in the morning, nothing had happened yet. I was in tremendous pain and the baby was ready to come out, but my body was not ready. The doctor said that they would have to perform a C-section. I told the doctor I did not want a C-section, but she said I had no choice.

As they prepared everything for the operation, I tried my martial arts breathing techniques. I was sure that if I used my martial arts ki op, or yell, I could push the baby out without a problem. However, to

Chook-Ok expecting her first daughter, Emerald.

my surprise, it didn't work that way. Then I touched my stomach and talked to baby Emerald inside me, "You need to come out now or I will need surgery. I want you to be born the natural way."

Suddenly, I felt that she was ready to come out and called the nurse. The nurse didn't believe me at first, but finally checked me at my insistence and said, "This baby is coming."

She called the doctor and within minutes Emerald was born. Barry was there and saw the whole thing. He clearly remembers the first thing I said when Emerald was born. I asked Barry, "Does she have ten fingers and ten toes?" He said yes and I relaxed. We named her Emerald Mi-Yong, which means "beautiful face."

On August 28, 1987 Emerald was born in Redwood City, California.

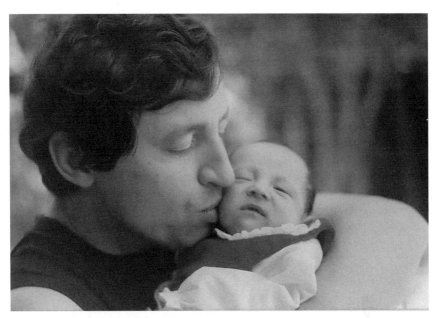

Barry fell in love with his daughter Emerald the moment she was born.

She was born one month early, but she was the cutest, loveliest baby girl you had ever seen. She had smooth brown hair and brown eyes. I was very happy to have a beautiful and healthy baby. And Barry? Well, from the moment Emerald was born, he was captivated by her. He held her in his arms right away; he talked to her, hugged her, and kissed her. He cared for her deeply. I observed his reaction intently and was relieved to see that he was not like my dad. He was and is a loving father who loves his daughter deeply. Life was good.

And life became more complicated. Now we had training, teaching, and parenting to combine in our already busy daily schedule. During Emerald's first three months, we did not take her to public places and asked visitors not to come over if they had a cold or another contagious illness to prevent Emerald from being exposed to it. It is a Korean tradition to wait three months for the baby to grow stronger before coming into contact with other people who might be ill.

I brought Emerald to the school with me; sometimes Choon-Up helped me care for her when I could not bring her along. I took Emerald with me almost everywhere I went, but I attended fewer demonstrations out of town.

I continued my training, which demanded more of my time than it did of Barry. It was a big challenge for me to learn the right sequence of movements. It was harder as I progressed in my training, because the forms and techniques were more advanced. I had to practice at least ten times longer than Barry. I struggled with my hand and foot movements. I had to concentrate to make sure I moved the right hand, not the left.

Other times, I reversed words, especially when I had to write down what people told me on the phone. I always had to double-check my spelling or phone numbers. I could not understand why this was happening to me. The first one to know my secret was Barry. He did not make a big deal out of it; he said he would help me practice when he could. I was very frustrated, but nothing was worse than Emerald getting sick.

Emerald's Illness

"Your daughter has leukemia. She needs to go to the hospital for further testing and treatment."

We were sitting at the doctor's office when she told us the news. She had cleared her schedule for the rest of the afternoon to discuss Emerald's latest blood test results with us: the troubling number of white blood cells in her blood sample.

This was not the first test Emerald had had. We had visited the pediatrician often because Emerald had a fever on and off for a couple of months. She had a high fever for two or three days, then she had a low-grade fever for several days, then the fever would increase again. Her temperature was not normal for months. The doctor explained to us that fever is usually the body's response to infection, to try to fight it off. During those months, the doctor had taken blood samples and determined the white blood cell count and looked for evidence of infection.

Emerald's white blood cell count was above normal for months. The highest count in her medical records was about seventy thousand. I was alarmed when I found out the normal values were between forty-five hundred and ten thousand. The day the pediatrician cleared her schedule to talk to us, she was very concerned. All the tests had come back negative for infection, which is the first suspect when the number of white blood cells is higher than normal.

The doctor explained to us that many times infections trigger an increase in white blood cells. For the body, an infection is like a foreign army invading a country. The body responds by recruiting its own army—the white blood cells—to fight and destroy the infection. White blood cells are always in the blood, but when there is an infection, the body recruits more white blood cells from internal organs like the spleen or lymph nodes to attack the invading infection.

Because this is the body's normal response, doctors usually look for an infection if a patient has a high white blood cell count. If the white blood cell count is high, but there is no direct evidence of infection, then doctors look for other causes for the high white blood cell count. There was one likely explanation for Emerald's high white blood cell count in the absence of infection—leukemia.

Our baby Emerald had leukemia? Blood cancer? Cancer is a hideous disease. It's a disease that's hard to fight, and a disease without a cure. Both of Barry's parents had other types of cancer and the disease took their lives. I told Barry that if I lost Emerald, I could not live any longer. I would follow her. I didn't want to live. I could not believe Emerald had leukemia.

Doctors told us that if Emerald had leukemia, she probably had a good chance of recovery, because children respond to treatment much better than adults. This was good news, but still we felt devastated. Our daughter had leukemia?

We were living in Fremont, but the hospital was in Redwood City, which is outside of San Francisco. It was about a thirty minute drive from Fremont to Redwood City and another thirty minutes to San Francisco from there. The doctor sent us to a large hospital in San Francisco for further testing. The doctor explained the tests to us.

In order to confirm or refute the diagnosis of leukemia, the doctor wanted to do a more precise test—a biopsy of the bone marrow. White blood cells are created in the marrow before traveling through the blood to the rest of the body. If Emerald's bone marrow had an unusually high white blood cell count, or the cells did not look like "normal" white blood cells, then her marrow was in overdrive, producing too many white blood cells and pouring them into the blood. This is leukemia. If her bone marrow looked normal, then Emerald did not have leukemia.

To perform the bone marrow biopsy, a doctor had to extract a sample of Emerald's bone marrow from her femur, the long leg bone, and study the marrow under the microscope.

We drove from Redwood City to the hospital in San Francisco, and the whole time, we were crying and praying. We cried and we cried silently while Emerald slept in the back seat until we arrived at the hospital.

Emerald was admitted into the hospital and Barry and I stayed with her. We didn't go home. I told Barry to go home to rest—to go back to the do jang. I would stay with Emerald. But he refused to leave. He brought a blanket and stayed with us, waiting for a diagnosis. What was going to happen to our baby? What would happen to our school? We thought we might have to close it until Emerald felt better. Life was very confusing; we just wanted to be with our daughter.

In the seven days we were at the hospital, doctors not only tested Emerald for leukemia, but for everything they could think of. They even did a spinal tap to check for meningitis in my tiny baby. For Barry and me, those seven days were a life-changing experience.

Every morning at five, a nurse would come to the room and draw blood from Emerald's little finger or from her tiny heel. And she would scream every time.

Every day was a test of our patience. We waited for the doctor to tell us the test results. Every day for seven days doctors told us the test results were negative and then planned another test for the next day. The nurse would come, prick Emerald's little finger, and she would scream. And we waited. They took so much blood from her. I don't know how she had enough blood to give every day.

The high fever appeared and disappeared, but there were no more symptoms. That was the only condition she had, but it would not go away. It was a medical mystery. The doctors also took blood samples from Barry and me and tested them side by side with Emerald's samples. We were also negative.

Of all the test results, the one we cared most about was the bone marrow biopsy. We still had hope that she might not have leukemia, but the doctor seemed so concerned that we were already devastated. When the results came, we could not believe it. Emerald did not have leukemia. Her bone marrow looked normal. We were overjoyed! What a relief after all the suffering, imagining Emerald had one of the worst diseases in the world. But if it was not leukemia, then what was it?

After seven days of daily testing, the doctors told us they could not find anything wrong in her little body. They had done all the tests available for any type of infection, even rare diseases, and all had come back negative. They had reached the point where there was nothing else to test. There was nothing else they could do for her. Her diagnosis was "fever of unknown origin."

They sent us home with instructions: "Give her this fever medicine when needed. Bring her back if new symptoms appear." We did not have a choice, so we went home. All the way back from San Francisco to Fremont, we cried quietly and prayed while Emerald slept in the back seat of the car. What was going to happen to our baby?

Family and friends asked us, "What does she have?" We told them that the doctors could not find anything wrong with her, and that they could not explain why she had a high fever or why it came and went. But she did not have leukemia, and we were thankful for that. We kept Emerald home when she had a high fever and tried to continue our working and training routine. My memories are quite blurry when I try to recall that time. We were worried and fearful all the time; we still did not know what was going to happen to our baby.

One day when she was ten months old, Emerald had a high fever; she was home, sleeping on a blanket over the carpet in the living room. Barry, who loves watermelon, brought a huge one to the kitchen nearby where Emerald was sleeping and cut it in half. He sat down on the floor by a short Korean-style table and began eating the juicy melon with a spoon. Emerald woke up. She saw her daddy eating watermelon and crawled toward him. She reached for the watermelon, grabbed a piece with her hand, and ate it. I just watched her; Barry just watched her. Emerald ate piece after piece of watermelon until she was full and then she stopped eating. I cleaned her up and she went back to sleep.

Barry and I looked at each other, wondering. She had never been interested in watermelon before. We checked her fever. She was still hot, and we let her sleep. A few hours later, she woke up and the fever was gone. She had not been fever-free for months! Would this be the end of it?

A few days passed, but the fever did not return. We looked at each other, wondering. Was she cured, or would the fever come back? A week passed, then two weeks, and the fever did not come back. It never came back again. I don't know what happened. The watermelon episode marked the end of her mysterious illness. Since that day, she has loved watermelon. If her dad had a piece of watermelon in his hand, she would come and take it. We don't know what happened, but everything went back to normal by itself.

Even though Emerald was about one year old when all this happened, it left an impression on her, like a subconscious, terrifying memory. For a long time after, Emerald had an intense fear of white coats. Even years after the incident, if anybody in a white coat walked toward her, she would either run away or start crying.

The experience also changed Barry and me. It emotionally scarred us. Being told that our daughter had leukemia left a permanent mark in our minds and hearts, even though later we knew it was not the case. Even now, I still get tears in my eyes just thinking about it.

We came out of this experience with a greater appreciation for our child. We do not take her for granted. It really struck us when we realized how fragile life is and that it can be gone in a split second and there is nothing you can do about it. That's still with us. I can't think of anything worse than having a child die before a parent.

In time, we returned to our usual routine of training and managing our school. We are very thankful that we did not have to close our school during the time Emerald was sick, and we have Master Richard R. and Master Joe F. to thank for it. They kept the school running smoothly while we had our attention focused on Emerald. Slowly, our lives returned to normal.

When Emerald turned one year old, we celebrated with the traditional One Year Old Birthday Ceremony. We celebrated at our school and invited family, friends, and our students to share this event with us. Guests brought her presents as in all birthday celebrations. This ceremony is not only to celebrate the baby's first year, but also to try to get a glimpse of what she will do when she grows up.

We placed a long and low Korean-style table on one side of the practice floor. Barry and I sat behind the table and our guests sat or stood in front of it. Emerald was sitting on Barry's lap. We were dressed in elegant Korean clothes to fit the occasion.

On the table, right in front of Emerald, there were three items: a one-dollar bill, a piece of thread, and a pencil. We had Emerald face the three objects and waited to see which one she would pick up. Tradition says that if the baby picks the one-dollar bill, she will be good at making money when she grows up. If she picks the thread, she will have a long life, and if she picks the pencil, she will be inclined towards an academic profession or the arts.

Emerald saw the three objects on the table and they caught her attention. She sat on her dad's lap with her back very straight and

Emerald's One Year Old ceremony.

placed both palms down on the table, looking curiously at the one -dollar bill, the piece of thread, and the pencil. Our friends, family, and students watched her make her decision. For a few seconds, nobody spoke or made any noise. What would she pick?

Emerald stretched her little arm toward the objects, opened her tiny hand, and picked up the pencil with her chubby fingers. Everybody clapped and cheered. Emerald kept the pencil in her tiny hands and played with it. That was her selection when she was one year old, and, as she grew up, she showed interest in dancing and music. She plays the saxophone, the piano, the guitar, and the Korean drums. She also sings and wants to have a career in music and acting.

Chapter 27

A Year in Korea

I can live in any place, at any time. I have no problem with that. What matters is that my husband, my children, and I are healthy and happy. There were things we wanted to do; we had goals, and we were working to reach them, no matter where we had to live to do so.

One of Barry's goals was to write a book about the origin and evolution of Korean Martial Arts. He wanted to gather first-hand information—primary sources—so we sold our school in San Mateo and moved to Pusan for one year. We still did not have much money and our way of living was extremely modest. It was poor, actually.

When we arrived in Pusan, we stayed at my brother's house for a few weeks, then we rented a small place on top of a street market. We had two tiny rooms, a small kitchen, and an outside bathroom. It smelled like

Choon-Ok and Barry focused on their advanced training.

market food—both the good and the bad smells—and sometimes it was quite noisy. But the way I looked at it, this home was an improvement compared to where I had lived when I was a little girl. It was our home, and it was better than a dressing room in our school in the United States.

I focused on training and caring for Emerald and our home. Barry also trained and used all his free time to do research for his book. We were doing what we wanted to do in that period of our life. But one day, we planned to have our own house in America.

Most people in Korea used to think that all Americans had plenty of money and lived in big houses with many rooms, a large kitchen, and private bathrooms, so when Barry's friend and his Korean wife visited us, she was shocked.

"Choon-Ok-ah, how can you live in a place like this? I cannot believe it!" she said.

I smiled. "This is a home, isn't it?" I replied. "We have two little rooms and a kitchen."

"I could not live this way," she said. "How can you do it?"

"I have no problem with that," I said. "I am happy, he's happy, and Emerald is happy. Everybody is happy, so there is no problem. We are continuing our training, and Barry is researching his book; we are doing what we want to do. This is only temporary."

I was also thinking, "You don't know it, but this is a better place than where I used to live when I was a little girl." I did not tell her that. I thought she would not understand my point of view, so I left it at that.

What counts to me is that we are happy inside. I have seen people whose homes are large and very nice looking. They wear elegant clothes and drive fancy cars, but inside they are unhappy and their lives fall apart. Couples get divorced and children take wrong turns in life. I did not want that in my life. I was lucky Barry and I had common goals and that we were pursuing them together.

Our friend's wife continued shaking her head and looking sad for us having to live in a place like this. Actually, many people in Korea live in small places until they make enough money to move to a house. But our friend's wife could not understand us. She thought that because I was married to an American I should live in a very nice place. She lived in a big house in Korea.

Korean culture allows for friends to tell each other things like, "How can you live in a place like this!" In Korea, we accept it; we might not like it, but we accept it because it is the truth. Barry and I accepted the place above the market. It was temporary. There was one thing that was the hardest to accept about the place, though. It had big cockroaches, and there was no way to get rid of them. We tried a few pest repellents and poisons, but they kept coming back. That's the worst part about living above a market—cockroaches live there, too.

The pests were worst at night time, when we were sleeping in our Korean-style bed, right on top of the floor. We could hear the cockroaches walking on the walls. We could hear the scratching of their legs and large, hard bodies against the wallpaper and the linoleum floors as they moved about the room. They crawled over us, too. I saw them on me more than once when I woke up at night. I brushed them away with my hand and tried to go back to sleep. I could have done without the cockroaches.

I told myself, "My child is having a better life than mine. She's never been hungry, or cold, or without medical attention when she needed it, like I was when I was a child. I want my future to be better than my past, better than when I was ten years old, and better than when I was a teenager. So far, we are doing better, but there is still plenty of room for improvement. One day, we will have a successful school training many students. One day, we will have a better home. We will continue working to reach our goals, step by step, with patience and perseverance."

Returning to America

Back in the United States, after a year living in Pusan, we had to prepare for a big move. Kuk Sa Nim had decided to move Kuk Sool Won headquarters to Houston, Texas. He wanted headquarters to be in a more central location than California, where they had been located since Kuk Sa Nim had opened his first school. We were still under his instruction, so if we wanted to continue our training, we had to move to Houston, too. We opened our first Houston school in 1991, in the Clear Lake area.

It takes time, patience, and a great deal of work to "raise" a school, much like it takes time to raise a child. It takes time to have a large group of students who enjoy practicing regularly. We wanted to teach Kuk Sool the traditional way—the way we had been taught since we began—but our experience in California had taught us that pure, traditional training was not compatible with American ways.

We had already seen some changes, some Kuk Sool adaptations to be more American-friendly, when we were living in California. While I was living in Korea before I was married, I had never seen Kuk Sa Nim teach students or demonstrate Kuk Sool techniques or forms in our school. Traditionally, only people loyal to a master and his school received instruction in martial arts, because martial arts meant power. Masters personally taught the secret art of self-defense only to their best students. In Korea, Kuk Sa Nim never demonstrated techniques or forms in public or even to lower-ranking students. He demonstrated or taught only high-ranking students privately.

I saw Kuk Sa Nim demonstrate advanced techniques and forms for the first time in a tournament in the United States. I was fascinated with his demonstration. He made it look effortless; it was second nature to him. The American students and the American spectators at the tournament did not know how lucky and privileged they were to be able to see Kuk Sa Nim perform. Watching him was a truly special treat for me. This had never happened in Korea. Some things began to change once Kuk Sool moved to the United States.

In Korea, my training was extremely intense, both physically and mentally. I trained for hours in hot weather or in cold weather. I trained on hard floors and practiced sparring without any sparring gear to protect my head, hands, feet, or shins. And when practicing sparring, everything was allowed. We could do take-downs, sweeping our opponent's legs with ours; we could punch, palm-strike, and kick full-force. If you got hit, too bad; you should have blocked the punch, the palm-strike, or the kick. That's why you practice blocking techniques for hours.

We were not allowed to ask our instructor to clarify how to do a technique; we had to observe him while he did it and imitate him. Sometimes our instructor only had time to show a move once, and it was our job to observe him intently and reproduce what he had done only once and very fast. If we dared to ask, we might get a stern reply. That's how traditional martial arts were taught in my time. It's the original way. If you are training on martial techniques, then you have to fight for real, fall for real, block strikes for real, and strike back for real.

Our instructors made sure we were constantly training, and that we did not give in to fatigue or shortness of breath. To keep us on task, they carried a stick made of bamboo called a jook-dae. It is actually a sword made of three small pieces of bamboo tied together into a sturdy yet flexible stick. As the instructors walked between the lines of practicing students, they whacked the jook-dae on the floor, making a loud slapping sound that could easily startle you, making sure you never stopped. Sometimes they whacked the stick against the back of our legs to keep us going if they noticed we were slowing down or running out of energy. And it worked. We focused on the exercise; we did not think about pain, breathlessness, or fatigue. We kept going.

The jook-dae was the perfect motivation to keep us training, no matter how tired we felt. And this was accepted as the best way of teaching martial arts. In the right measure, it was not considered abuse or disrespect. The instructor was there to teach us; he had to make sure we did our best during the training. We did not question the instructor; we followed his orders and practiced until he told us to stop.

Many of these teaching approaches, we realized, had to change when Kuk Sool came to America. American culture is different from Korean culture. What we consider strict, disciplined training is frowned upon in America. Not many American students would stay long in traditional Korean training, not because they do not have the physical or mental endurance, but because traditional teaching methods are not considered appropriate. They could be considered abusive and even cause legal problems. Kuk Sool teaching had to change and adapt to a different way of thinking in the new world.

In our schools in America, Barry and I teach differently than we have been taught. We are more patient with our students, both children and adults. We repeat techniques and forms a few times instead of just once. We welcome questions from our students and have extra classes and private lessons for those wishing for more practice or review. None of this was available during my traditional training.

We offer protective gear to students during sparring practice, and it is mandatory to use a mouth piece to protect the teeth from a hard punch or kick to the mouth. Students have the option to purchase and use their personal protective gear. They cannot spar without it. I did not have any of that as a student.

For junior students, we sometimes combine kicking, punching, or falling drills with games that will keep their energy going and enhance their training. They jump over obstacles before kicking or do relay races in teams. We give instructions in loud voices, such as commands calling to immediate attention posture, or calling for particular kicking or punching techniques. We don't raise our voices at our students; we correct mistakes in a constructive way. In time, the adaptations to the American, Western way has attracted many students to our school and to many other martial arts schools in America and around the world. Kuk Sool has grown immensely worldwide since Kuk Sa Nim established it in Korea in 1958.

By 1993, our Clear Lake School had grown into a solid business and we bought our first home. It was a one-story, three-bedroom, two-bath home that was big enough to add a new member to our family. It was in this home that I slept in my first American-style bed. For thirteen years, ever since we had been married, I had wanted an American-style bed, but Barry would not accept it. He loves Korean-style beds, and he would not have any other style. I had to wait thirteen years until Barry agreed to have an American bed.

A few years later, we sold our first home and bought our second house. It was a two-story home located in the suburbs close to the school. We had five bedrooms, a large kitchen, a living room area, and even a pool in our backyard. We had come a long way from living in the dressing room of our first school.

Life was still very busy, but it was more relaxed. We enjoyed a bit more free time, and one of the things Barry and I like to do together is ride a motorcycle. He has been riding it since before we were married; he had told me in his letters. Now I enjoyed riding with him very much. Life was a bit easier and we were happy our second daughter, Jada, was on her way.

Chapter 28

Early Delivery

I was about thirty-three weeks pregnant with our second daughter Jada, and all had gone well until that morning. The day began as it usually did: I drove Emerald to school and returned home to exercise. On the way back home, I had an uncomfortable feeling in the upper, right side of my abdomen, accompanied by a bit of nausea. I thought it was because of a heavy lunch I had eaten the day before. Was it food poisoning? It was hard to pinpoint the feeling. At that moment, I just had a tiny bit of pain, but mostly I felt strange, uncomfortable; it was not normal. I did not feel dizzy, and had neither a headache nor any sharp pain anywhere, just an odd feeling I had not experienced before. It didn't feel right, but I did not give it too much importance at the time. I lay down on my bed when I arrived home. I told Barry I had an uncomfortable feeling in my stomach. I was hoping it would disappear after I rested for an hour or two.

The odd feeling did not go away. Barry called the doctor. She asked us to go to her office right away. We arranged for a friend to pick up Emerald from school and care for her while we headed to the doctor's office, which was about forty-five minutes from home, near downtown Houston.

In the office, the doctor checked my blood pressure and other vital signs. It seemed I just had gastritis—an inflammation in the stomach caused by something I ate—but it did not seem serious at the moment. The doctor sent me home with instructions to call her if I felt worse. I did feel much worse. The following week, I had a constant headache and my stomach hurt all the time, especially after eating. I could barely eat because of the pain. My blood pressure was extremely high. The doctor was very concerned. She asked us to go to the hospital immediately.

I did not understand at the moment the severity of the situation, but if the doctor wanted me to go in the hospital I knew my "weird stomach feeling" was something to pay attention to. I was admitted at the Woman's Hospital of Texas that same afternoon. I wondered how long I would have to stay. I was not fully prepared for the arrival of the new baby yet.

Examinations continued in the hospital. They took my blood pressure, did an ultrasound to check on the baby, and drew blood to see how some of my organs were working—they mentioned the kidneys and the liver.

After a few hours, I asked Barry, "Are we going home today?"

He said in a neutral tone, "No, we are staying here."

"There is a problem, right?" I asked him. He said the doctor would come and talk to us when all the tests were finished and she had the report of a consult she had requested from a colleague. We waited. I just wanted to go home.

The doctor came into the room and talked to us. I did not understand all the medical details very well, but Barry told me the bottom line.

"What is the problem?" I asked.

"The doctors say they have to deliver the baby. Right now," said Barry. His face was not neutral any more. He was concerned. "They have to do it now. If we wait much longer the baby may suffer. And you, too. It's an emergency. They want to do a C-section."

It was a simple decision for me. If the doctor thought the baby was in danger and the solution was to deliver her right now, then I would. "Let's do it," I said. While they prepared all that was needed for the baby's delivery, Barry went home to gather clothes and other things I would need while I stayed at the hospital. I had not packed for the hospital yet; I had thought that I had plenty of time, because I was only in my seventh month. Barry had to pack a week's worth of clothes and other necessities for me.

I was worried. We had not finished preparing everything at home to welcome the new baby. I had not finished fixing her crib, her room, and her clothes. At the moment, however, that did not seem important. I still did not know why the baby had to be delivered in such a rush and how that related to my stomach feeling strange.

The anesthesiologist gave me an epidural, not complete anesthesia. I was somehow aware of what was going on, but not too much. Barry was allowed in the operating room and he watched the procedure. It was not an easy thing for him to do. His wife and daughter were going through an emergency surgery.

"I did not feel queasy, but I did not look inside her body. She is my wife," he said about the experience. "I stepped back and watched the doctor bring my baby into the world."

He told me later that he saw when our baby emerged from the womb, pulled out so carefully by the doctor. His first thought was, "She's like a Barbie doll; she's so small and thin." There was no meat on her. He said he could have held her in the palm of one hand. She was only two pounds, seven ounces. "I could not believe how small she was," he told me. Little though she was, she began crying—more like screaming—right away. This was a good sign. The baby was small, but healthy. That's all I cared about. We named our second daughter Jada Mi-Ho. Her name means "beautiful tiger."

Jada was in good health, but she was premature. The medical chart said, "The baby looked vigorous, but was small." The doctors said she had to spend time in an incubator to continue her growth and gain weight before she could go home. She stayed in the Neonatal Intensive Care Unit for thirty-three days. We visited her every single day she was there.

They brought me back to my room and told me I was expected to recover in a few days. I recovered well; after eight days in the hospital, we went home without Jada. It was one of the hardest things I had ever had to do.

The entire time I was in the hospital, Barry did not explain anything to me; he just told me what the doctors wanted to do. I only knew that the odd feeling in my stomach meant the baby was in danger and that I needed emergency surgery to deliver Jada prematurely. A few days after the surgery, I began to feel better. The stomach pain and the headaches went away, and my blood pressure began to return to normal. I did not think much about me, just about Jada.

Once we were at home, Barry revealed the complete story behind Jada's birth. The night I was admitted into the hospital, the doctors told Barry that my body was reacting negatively to the baby. I had HELLP syndrome, and the reason it happens to some women during pregnancy is still a mystery. I had all the typical symptoms of HELLP: "H" for hemolysis, or breakage of red blood cells; "EL" for elevated liver enzymes; and "LP" for low platelet count. I also had high blood pressure caused by the pregnancy. Basically, I was losing the vital red blood cells that feed my body oxygen, my liver and kidneys were shutting down, and my platelets were diminishing, which put me at risk of bleeding uncontrollably, because platelets take care of coagulation.

Most dangerous was the elevated blood pressure. In the hospital, it reached 150/103 (normal is 120/80). The doctor told Barry it was so high that they were concerned I might have a stroke, a heart attack, or that the placenta might rupture. They were actually surprised I had not had any of those episodes yet. They said I probably had not had a stroke or a heart attack yet, because I was very fit due to my regular training. My heart was strong, but for how long? Jada and I had to be separated immediately or I might die.

Besides what my body was going through, Jada was also suffering. The doctor told us that she had IUGR, which stands for Intrauterine Growth Restriction. This meant that my body was not nurturing Jada well enough to support her normal growth. At thirty-three weeks of gestation, Jada was below the tenth percentile, or very small for her age. We had both been in a life-threatening situation.

I knew all this after I was back at home, out of danger, and my liver, kidneys, and blood pressure were back to normal. Barry, on the other hand, had to live through the uncertainties of what would happen next. And he didn't tell me. Would my body recover after Jada and I were separated or not? After fifteen years, when my husband recalls this incident, he relives it intensely, as if time has not passed. He spared me the worries of my own fate. Instead, my memories are of Jada and her own recovery from being born early and my constant fear she might have lasting effects from her birth.

Going home without our newborn baby was heartbreaking for both of us. Leaving my tiny daughter in an incubator when I had to go home was hard to cope with. We cried in silence on our way home.

We visited her every day for as long as it was possible. Every day, after we dropped Emerald at school, I rushed Barry: "Let's go, let's go. Let's go see Jada." Every day as we walked into the hospital, we had only one thought in our minds: "How did she spend the night? Is everything OK with Jada?" Every day we found her well, healthy, and slowly gaining weight. We relived this situation every day for thirty-three days.

We had to wear long-sleeved surgical gowns before we could get close to Jada. We tied the gown around the waist and it would cover all of our clothes. We learned to wash hands correctly. Up to then, Barry and I thought we knew how to wash our hands, but we really did not know how to do it right. One of the nurses showed us how to do it properly before we could touch Jada.

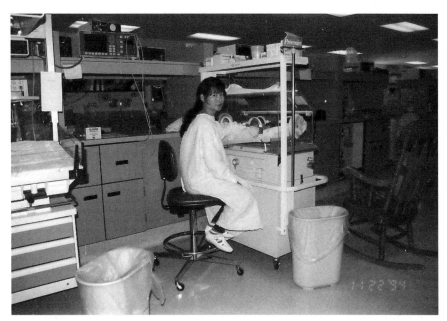

Choon-Ok caressing Jada in the incubator.

We rolled our sleeves above the elbow and rinsed our hands and forearms with warm water. Then we used a bar of disinfectant soap to scrub and scrub every inch of our hands and forearms. Every crevice, the spaces between fingers, all around the forearm, an inch of skin at a time—we scrubbed once, rinsed, then scrubbed and rinsed again. We dried our hands and forearms with a clean towel. I had never taken so much time to wash my hands, but that was how you had to do it before you could touch your premature baby.

We could touch her with our clean, bare hands, hold her, and feed her. Sometimes she opened her eyes and seemed to look at us; sometimes she was sleeping peacefully in my arms. I sat on a chair and held her for hours. Barry would extend his left hand over her back or chest and focused on giving her "Ki," internal power energy to help her gain strength. He gave Jada Ki every day. Today I tell him, "You gave Jada too much Ki!" She's hot all the time while Emerald is cold all the time.

When I saw Jada at birth, she was very tiny and helpless. How is this possible? How can she be so little? At the same time, she was healthy, and that was good enough for me. The doctors expected her to grow normally, but they were concerned she might have complications later in life because she was born early.

Barry and Choon-Ok spent most of the day with Jada while she was in intensive care.

Jada might have breathing problems, because her lungs had not developed fully at the time of the emergency surgery. She might also have eye problems. Being born premature increased her chances of suffering from health problems as she grew up. I later saw quite a few children with breathing or eye problems because they were premature. Would Jada be one of them? We were constantly on alert for any indication of any problems. Even normal childhood illnesses most parents don't worry about excessively were a serious concern for us.

When Jada was a few months old and already back home, she caught chicken pox from her sister, Emerald, who was about seven years old. For most parents, it's not a problem to have all their children go through chicken pox at the same time. Some have told me they prefer it this way, because they are done with chicken pox all at once. But Jada was still small for her age, weighing less than four pounds, and we were—and still are—on high alert whenever she got sick. We worried about her when we saw the first red spots on her tiny face and detected a mild fever.

We were also worried about Emerald. After she was cured of the "fever of unknown origin," she had been a healthy baby. She was now going through chicken pox, like most other kids do, but for us chicken pox

Jada's One Year Old Ceremony. She cried often to her parents' despair.

was a red alert. We took both girls to the doctor, we watched them all the time, and we measured their temperature. We made sure they had plenty to drink and eat and jumped from our seats if they cried or complained. We worried more than was necessary. We know it, but we can't help it sometimes. Both our girls recovered fine, like most children do.

One thing that was very hard on us was listening to Jada's long crying spells. She would cry constantly. Sometimes, she would cry for an hour straight and we did not know why. We changed her diapers, but she would still cry. We would feed her; she would cry. We would rock her, walk her, and drive around the neighborhood to calm her. But she would still cry and cry. We were told that when a baby cries for an hour or more, something is wrong. We lived on the edge for many nights in a row. We asked friends, family, and the doctor. Jada was fine; she just cried a lot. This was very hard to deal with. At the same time, she gained weight, she developed as expected, and she laughed. She was a healthy baby and she has grown up into a healthy young woman. She just didn't stop crying.

All that constant crying got on our nerves; it exhausted us. We are so thankful to Master Terry H. because she helped us deal with Jada's

Choon-Ok and Jada during her One Year Old Ceremony.

crying spells. Master Terry would come to our home after a day at work and see us sitting on the sofa, feeling exhausted, staring into the distance, and barely saying hello to her. She would take crying Jada in her arms and slowly walk around the house, holding Jada in front of her, showing her the pictures on the walls and talking soothingly to her. She would feed her, change her diaper, and rock her. We knew Jada was in very good hands, so we went to our bedroom, closed the door, and rested. Master Terry's help was a life saver; it gave us the break we needed to recover our strength.

Jada eventually overcame her crying spells and continued growing normally. During her One Year Old Ceremony, she also picked the pencil, just as her sister Emerald had done years before. Barry and I are looking forward to what she will pursue when she grows up.

Our daughters have both given us big health-related scares. Emerald was ten months old when she got sick with a "fever of unknown origin" and then recovered on her own. Jada did not wait that long; she was not even born when we thought we might lose her. Those experiences have scarred us in the sense that we are on the alert when either Emerald or Jada get sick. We realize that it's mostly in our minds; our daughters are healthy and strong and live normal lives like other girls their age. Still, we cannot help it but worry so much about them.

The experience with Jada has even influenced how I discipline her. When Emerald was a little girl and she disobeyed me, I punished her in the traditional Korean style. She had to kneel and raise her arms above her head for ten or fifteen minutes. She would cry and complain that her arms hurt and that her knees hurt. I did not give in. I let her complain until the time was up. But when Jada disobeyed me, I could not bring myself to punish her that way. I could not do it. I would remember how helpless and small she was when she was in the incubator, when I held her in my arms and she was no bigger than a Barbie doll. I could not punish her that way.

Of course, Emerald complained. "Why don't you punish Jada the same way you punish me?" she would ask me when she saw Jada get away with disobeying me. "I just can't." Life works in mysterious ways.

Chapter 29

Of Dog Rules and Riding Horses

After Jada came home from the hospital, I felt complete; we were all together and life moved on. Our martial arts school continued growing, the children continued growing, and our training brought us closer to our life-long goal of receiving the highest rank in Kuk Sool Won—Ninth Degree Black Belt. It was about this time that my daughters each wanted a dog. "A dog?" I said. "I don't want a dog in the house!"

The childhood memory of my dog Nabi persisted in my mind. I had raised Nabi in Koje Do from the time he was a puppy. Mom had sold him and made Nabi soup; it was one of the worst experiences of my life. I had decided then that I was not going to suffer from another loss like Nabi's. I was not going to get attached to another animal. But my daughters wanted a dog, and I had to deal with them somehow.

I was not in favor at the beginning, but after thinking about it and talking to Barry, I realized that my sad experience with Nabi was not a reason for my daughters not to have their own dog. In the end, I decided my daughters could have a dog, but we sat down and set some "dog rules" first:

1. They stay outside the house at all times, either in the backyard or the garage. They do not come inside the house.

2. My daughters (each one has her own dog) will feed them, clean up after them, bathe them, and make sure they have enough water. I will feed them sometimes if necessary.

3. I am not going to touch the dogs. If I have to block them from running inside the house, I will raise my feet in front of them; I will not use my hands. They will learn to avoid my feet.

4. If they run away when the gate is open, I will call them but not go after them. They have learned to come back quickly when I call them, and run to the garage, avoiding my feet completely.

5. They will wear a collar all the time so I can grab them by it and guide them outside if I have to. I don't want to touch the dogs.

I changed rule #1 recently, because Houston can get too hot and humid in the summer for the dogs to spend a long time outdoors. I allow them to stay inside the house in certain areas closed off by gates, like the kitchen. But at the first sign of trouble, like barking or jumping on a visitor, they will go out.

I determined not to get attached to the dogs or any other pet my daughters wanted. The rules continue to work well to this day, but in time I got a little bit attached to the dogs. They are cute and not so bad after all. I feel comfortable having them around me. My "dog rules" still stand though.

In 2002, Kuk Sa Nim told Barry and me that he wanted us to learn to ride a horse and perform horseback archery. It is not part of the regular curriculum for Ninth Degree Black Belt, but Kuk Sa Nim wanted to preserve this martial arts tradition and he asked us to learn it. My first thought was "That's impossible!" But, Barry said, "Yes, sir."

Kuk Sa Nim stands with Choon-Ok and Barry.

Barry and I went to the stables next to Kuk Sa Nim's ranch and Barry signed up for one month of horseback riding lessons. The instructor, Laura, was very kind and helpful. I just listened and watched Barry.

He asked Laura, "Do you think I can learn to do archery on horseback while the horse is running in about ten lessons?"

She looked at Barry like he had lost his mind. "Let's start practicing, and we'll see how it goes," she said.

During the month Barry took horseback riding lessons, I watched him from a distance. For the whole month, I kept asking Kuk Sa Nim, "Do I have to?" Kuk Sa Nim nodded. I did not know how to face this challenge. I did not want to touch any animal, but I would have to touch the horse if I was going to ride it. I just did not want to do it.

Before he rode the horse—whose name was Lakota—Barry brushed him to help both of them get used to each other. Even from far away, I could smell the horse and I did not like the smell. I did not want to touch the horse. I kept asking Kuk Sa Nim, "Do I have to do it?" Kuk Sa Nim always nodded. I did not want to brush a horse or feel its sweaty coat or clean up after it.

Barry did not try to convince me to do it. He asked, "Will you try today?" I always replied, "I do not want to do it!" We went to the stables together and I watched him handle the horse, ride the horse, and move on to archery while riding the horse.

I asked Kuk Sa Nim one more time, "Do I have to do it?"

This time he looked at me. "Yes! You have to do it!" he told me. That was it; he had given me an order and I had no way around it. I had to do it or I would not progress in my training.

I set my mind to it. I told myself, "I have to do it! I will do it." I put aside the barriers I had raised against animals since I was a little girl. I went to horseback riding class and did not let my aversion stop me. I let Laura guide me through the steps of handling the horse; I also rode Lakota. I just did what she said without thinking of anything else. I grabbed the reins and guided Lakota out of the stable, slowly. I did not look at him. I tied him to the fence, and brushed him slowly and softly, as Laura had told me. Lakota stayed calm. We seemed to tolerate each other well as lessons progressed.

After we learned basic riding, Juliana, who is also a student of ours and a horse whisperer, invited us to come ride at her ranch. She said she had two horses that would be perfect for horseback archery. Their names were Cody and Brown Ears. They were already trained for riding

Choon-Ok and Barry during formal horseback archery practice.

with weapons, because she rode them practicing Western-style jousting. Cody and Brown Ears did not fear the weapons around them or the sounds those weapons might make. We just had to work with them to gain their trust.

I learned to saddle Cody and to ride him. I did not allow myself any other thoughts but following the steps Juliana had laid down for me. I rode him, and it worked. After about a month following Juliana's routine, I was riding Cody and practicing archery from horseback. I also learned sword fighting from horseback, and it was not as bad as I had imagined it would be. I went through the motions, following the process step by step, and it worked. I believe that whatever you tell your mind you have to do, you will do.

Barry and I practiced together following Kuk Sa Nim's training and, one day, he asked us to dress in our most formal uniform, which is reserved for special occasions, like promotions or public demonstrations. The occasion this time was that the Korean Broadcasting System, the Korean national TV station based in Seoul, was coming to

Kuk Sa Nim's ranch to film us practicing horseback archery and sword fighting. They showed the documentary in Korea. It was the first time this level of training was available for public viewing.

Now, I am very comfortable around horses. I love Cody. I still don't like other animals, but I do get along well with horses. I brush Cody and I clean his feet so they stay healthy. I even clean up after him. His smell still bothers me, especially his "waste products," but I just focus on the task, not the smell, and get it done. For forty years I was not close to animals—I did not want to be—and the first time I broke that forty-year-old barrier was with a horse. I would never have thought that would happen to me.

I became so comfortable around horses that one day Barry and I decided to race. We were at Juliana's ranch with her horses, Jabar and Brown Ears. Cody, my usual horse, did not like to run so I was riding Jabar instead. The day was nice, but it had been raining earlier and some paths were slightly muddy. We were enjoying a nice, slow ride when Barry had a head start and began galloping. I was going to fol- low at a canter, which is a slower gait, but my horse Jabar did not seem to like the idea of Brown Ears getting ahead of him. He decided to gallop after Brown Ears and at first I thought of holding him back, but then I changed my mind. "You want to race?" I asked Jabar. "Let's do it!" It looked like fun. Jabar darted forward, chasing Brown Ears. I held on tight to the reins with my hands and to his body with my legs. The wind was blowing on my face. The speed was exhilarating. "Let's go, Jabar!"

He wanted to pass Brown Ears so desperately that he took a side path, running past the other horse. But the path was still wet and slip- pery. Jabar slipped to his knees and I was thrust forward over his head. My immediate reaction was to roll on the ground, as I had done thou- sands of time during training, to fall in a way I would not get hurt. I couldn't do it this time. My foot got caught on the stirrup and I was stuck with Jabar for a split second. Everything happened very quickly. My horse did not fall; he recovered his balance and kept on running. My foot got free of the stirrup and I flew toward the ground. I did not have time to curl my body to roll; I just had time to tuck my arms against my body, bending my elbows and hitting the ground hard on my shoulder.

I was lucky. I only had a few bruises, but the fall had knocked the wind out of me. Barry had seen me fall and hurried toward me. He saw I was gasping for air and reacted quickly. He dropped from his horse and ran toward me. He grabbed my shoulders, put his knee in the middle of my back and pulled my arms backwards. I felt the air rush back into my lungs. I could breathe again. I laughed nervously. It had been a close call. I knew it could have been much worse. Would I ride again? Of course. Why not? Now that I had overcome my fear of horses, I was not going back.

Chapter 30

The Little Girl on the Beach Smiles

I did not let my difficulties during training—which made me practice harder and longer than other students—stop me from reaching the highest degree in Kuk Sool Won. My struggles were a mystery to me, and I have only recently found an explanation for them.

I mentioned the problem casually to one of my instructors, Ann S., who is a teacher. She said, "I have a few kids in my school who have the same problem. They have been diagnosed with dyslexia." She explained to me that people with dyslexia have some areas of their brain wired differently, and that's why they see letters or words in reverse when reading or writing. Sometimes they have problems like I do with my hand techniques.

It seems that my student's assessment might explain my difficulties. For me, extra practice was the only thing that helped me overcome it. It was reassuring to learn about this problem; I was not dumb. I am glad I ignored those words and persisted in my training.

In October 2008, Barry and I received our promotion to Ninth Degree Black Belt. We have reached a major goal in our martial arts careers. On this date, Kuk Sa Nim, Kuk Sool Won Grand Master, promoted us to the highest level in Kuk Sool. Our titles are now Su Suhk Kwang Jang Nim for Barry, and Su Suhk Yuh Kwang Jang Nim for me. I have become the first woman of any nationality to achieve the highest level in Kuk Sool Won and Barry has become the first American man to reach the highest rank in Kuk Sool Won.

We have reached this point in our careers after years of constant training and testing. We had to combine our training with family affairs, some of which were extremely intense and meant more than training itself, like Emerald's mysterious illness and Jada's premature birth.

Reaching the highest ranking in Kuk Sool Won was a life-long goal for both Barry and me, and we are deeply pleased to have reached this point in our lives. Our school students were very happy for us, too.

Kuk Sool's Iron Butterfly.

One of our students, Carol P., surprised me with a wonderful gift. She had arranged for a Houston hibiscus expert to create a new variety of this beautiful flower and name it after me: "Kuk Sool's Iron Butterfly." Grand Master and Chief Master called me "iron butterfly" because I am strong yet feminine. The new hibiscus variety has a delicate pink and white color and the flowers are quite large. I am very thankful for such a special gift and I have a few of the plants in my own backyard.

With our promotion to Ninth Degree Black Belt, we have reached a major milestone, which makes me think about what we have today. Among all the ups and downs, we managed to raise our school in Clear Lake, Houston. We have about three hundred students currently enrolled and they are like a big family to us. They are enthusiastic about their training, and they have supported the school through many tournaments. Thanks to them, our Clear Lake school has been awarded the title of Top School in national and international Kuk Sool Won tournaments. We moved in 2005 to a bigger locale just a mile from our original Houston school. Now we have a large, outdoor area we use to practice archery and other techniques. Our school is successful.

As I work on my memoir, I can see not only what I have achieved, but also the journey that brought me to where I am today. I can see how my life has changed from the time when I was a little girl on the beach of Koje Do. If I gather my memories and place them on a time-line and watch them in fast forward, I see my life flow in front my eyes, changing for the better. This is what I see:

It all began on a cold day when I was born to a sea woman, a hae-nyo, a real-life mermaid, diving in the ocean. The baby grew into a little girl, who wandered on the beach of a small village, helpless, but deeply wanting to change her life, a life filled with hunger, cold days and nights, hand-me-down clothes, and a father who was not caring. She was as delicate and graceful as a butterfly.

The girl moved to a city where she discovered her personal passion, the martial art of Kuk Sool Won. It gave her focus, it gave her physical and mental strength, and it gave her hope and the means to change her life—the life of the little girl on the beach—for better.

The little girl never planned for this; the opportunities came to her and she made choices. She knew what she did *not* want. She did not want to live the life of a traditional Korean woman, but she wanted a family. She wanted to dedicate her life to Kuk Sool, as she had prom-ised Chief Master she would.

The opportunity came to move to America, where women could have their wishes heard, where a woman could be first, and she, no longer a little girl, chose to come to America and marry an American Kuk Sool student. They faced challenges to their wish of becoming masters; they endured opposition from many people, including their own families. They continued their training and had support from Kuk Sa Nim.

They became masters: she became the first woman to be promot-ed to master level and he was the first non-Korean man to achieve the same rank. They had little money but a clear goal. And they wanted to go all the way. Why not? It seemed the right thing to do—to continue their training and personal improvement. Amid opposition, family illness, and with little money, they pursued and achieved their goal.

They have their own school, which is very successful. They don't live in the dressing room anymore. They have their own home in a Houston suburb. They are together and their children are healthy. They have

Choon-Ok, Barry, Jada (center), and Emerald in a Texas bluebonnet field in 2009.

both achieved the highest rank in Kuk Sool Won. Choon-Ok, a mermaid's daughter, is still a butterfly, but she's now an Iron Butterfly.

The little girl on the beach has fulfilled her dream. I imagine she lifts her eyes from the sand she's poking with a stick and looks at me. She smiles. She bows. She thanks me: "Kam sa hanm ni da!"

Appendix

Favorite Korean and American Recipes

Cucumber Salad (Korea)
Serves 5

3 medium-sized cucumbers
3 green onions, chopped

Dressing
½ cup soy sauce
⅓ cup white vinegar
1 tbsp. sesame oil
2 tbsp. sugar
1 tsp. minced garlic
1 tbsp. sesame seeds

Peel cucumbers and slice them about ¼-inch thick. Place cucumbers in serving bowl.

Slice green onions to about the same thickness as the cucumbers. Set them aside.

To prepare the dressing, mix the soy sauce, vinegar, sesame oil, sugar, garlic, sesame seeds, and green onions in a large jar. Cover and shake to mix well.

Add dressing on top of cucumbers and mix well with a spoon.

Kimchi (Korea)
Serves 60

7 medium-sized Napa cabbages

3 bundles of large green onions, sliced ¼-inch thick
⅓ cup sweet rice flour
1 ¼ cups water
½ cup fish sauce
1 ½ cups hot pepper
1 large pear (can be substituted with 1 tsp. sugar)
3 generous tbsp. minced garlic
½ tsp. sesame seeds
Salt

Cut cabbage in quarters and slice into bite-sized pieces, discarding hard white ending. Place in kitchen sink and wash well with tap water.

Take bunches of cabbage with your hands and transfer to a large bowl, draining off the excess water before transferring. Add salt generously. Transfer another bunch to the bowl and add salt. Continue until all the cabbage has been transferred to the bowl. Leave at room temperature for about 2 hours for cabbage to absorb the salt.

While the cabbage absorbs the salt, in a medium-sized pan, combine rice flour with 1½ cups of water, mixing well with whisk. Turn heat on high and stir constantly with spoon until mixture thickens. Remove from heat.

Add fish sauce and mix with green onions.

Add hot pepper. Mix well. Set aside.

Mix the pear cut into pieces, garlic, and ¼ cup of water in a blender. Add this mixture to the hot pepper sauce and mix well with a spoon. Add sesame seeds. Set aside at room temperature.

After cabbage is salted, rinse three times with tap water. After the last rinse, place in a large strainer for 30 minutes to drain off excess water. Transfer half the cabbage to a large bowl and add half the sauce, mixing well with hands (use clear plastic gloves) until all the cabbage is covered with the sauce. Store in a large glass jar and refrigerate. Eat mixed with white rice.

Banana Pudding
Serves 10

1 box of vanilla wafers (12 oz.)
2 boxes of vanilla pudding mix (3.12 oz. box)

10 medium-sized, ripe bananas sliced about ¼ inch thick.
Milk, to meet instructions on pudding box

Cover the bottom of a large, round serving bowl with a single layer of wafers, side by side. Place a single layer of sliced bananas on top of wafer layer. Continue alternating layers of wafers and bananas until almost reaching the rim of bowl, ending with wafers.

Prepare pudding mix according to box instructions.

Pour over wafers and bananas while still hot.

Let cool down at room temperature for about 30 minutes, then refrigerate covered with plastic wrap.

Haenyo, the Sea Women

Female divers of Korea and Japan have been harvesting the ocean for at least fifteen hundred years. In Korea, archeological research has revealed that the tradition began before the fourth century as a way to gather pearls. Later on it became focused on gathering food. At the beginning men dived also, but later on they were completely replaced by women.

Haenyo, who are also called "jamsu" or "ama" in Korea, are capable of diving very deep with a single breath. Some have reported diving to about eighty feet (twenty-four meters), and holding their breaths for up to two minutes. In warm weather, they work four hours every day and rest away from the water for an hour. In winter, they dive less often. Haenyo dive most of the year and rest for a month. Before wetsuits were available, these "mermaids" dove wearing only cotton trunks, shirts, and goggles. Since 1977, most mermaids wear wet suits which keep them warmer longer, allowing them to dive more often. Being a Haenyo is a life-long profession. Many start at twelve years old and dive until they are sixty-five, or as long as their health permits. The job is difficult, but it also offers the women independence. On Korean islands, Haenyo became the breadwinners.

Han Rim Hwa, a researcher of Cheju Island's traditional culture at the Institute for Peace Studies at Cheju National University, indicates that in the late 1980s, Haenyo "lived and worked in tightly knit communities. On the outside, they don't look that different from other islanders, but if you look inside, they are so different." The Haenyo are a close group of friends and relatives who share their days and livelihood together.

Unfortunately, the tradition is fading. Statistics from the Korean maritime and fisheries organizations indicate that the number of registered Haenyo has declined dramatically. In 1965, there were twenty-three thousand Haenyo in Cheju Island, Korea's largest island. This number represents one-fifth of the female population older than fifteen. In 2002, there were 5,659 Haenyo registered, of which 39 percent were in their sixties, and the oldest member was eighty-seven. There were only two Haenyo age thirty or younger—the youngest was twenty-seven. The Haenyo population has declined because the economy has changed and diving has become difficult. Korean women today have other options to reach economic independence. For many, however, Haenyo are still the symbol of Cheju and other Korean islands.

Further Reading

Charr, Easurk Emsen. *The Golden Mountain: The Autobiography of a Korean Immigrant, 1895-1960.* 2d ed. Chicago: University of Illinois Press, 1961.

Lee, Mary Paik and Sucheng Chan. *Quiet Odyssey: A Pioneer Korean Woman in America.* Seattle : University of Washington Press, 1990.

Harmon, R. Barry. *5,000 years of Korean Martial Arts: The Heritage of the Hermit Kingdom Warriors.* Indianapolis: Dog Ear Publishing, 2007.

Tse, Helen. *Sweet Mandarin: The Courageous True Story of Three Generations of Chinese Women and Their Journey from East to West.* New York: Thomas Dunne Books, 2007.

World Kuk Sool Association "Traditional Korean Martial Arts—Kuk Sool Won." Last modified 2010. http://www.kuksoolwon.com/history01.html

Index